Bail support schemes for adults

Anthea Hucklesby

First published in Great Britain in 2011 by The Policy Press

The Policy Press
University of Bristol
Fourth Floor, Beacon House
Queen's Road
Bristol BS8 1QU
UK

t: +44 (0)117 331 4054
f: +44 (0)117 331 4093
tpp-info@bristol.ac.uk
www.policypress.co.uk

North American office:
The Policy Press
c/o International Specialized Books Services
920 NE 58th Avenue, Suite 300
Portland, OR 97213-3786, USA
t: +1 503 287 3093
f: +1 503 280 8832
info@isbs.com

© The Policy Press 2011

ISBN 978 1 84742 954 4

British Library Cataloguing in Publication Data
A catalogue record for this report is available from the British Library.

Library of Congress Cataloging-in-Publication Data
A catalog record for this report has been requested.

The right of Anthea Hucklesby to be identified as author of this work has been asserted by her in accordance with Sections 77 and 78 of the Copyright, Designs and Patents Act 1988.

The statements and opinions contained within this publication are solely those of the authors and not of the University of Bristol or The Policy Press. The University of Bristol and The Policy Press disclaim responsibility for any injury to persons or property resulting from any material published in this publication.

The Policy Press works to counter discrimination on grounds of gender, race, disability, age and sexuality.

Cover design by Qube Design Associates, Bristol
Printed in Great Britain by Hobbs, Southampton

FSC
www.fsc.org
MIX
Paper from
responsible sources
FSC® C020438

Contents

List of figures and tables

Figures

Tables

Acknowledgements

The Effective Bail Scheme process evaluation included in this report was funded by the Ministry of Justice and carried out at the Centre for Criminal Justice Studies, University of Leeds. The research team consisted of Anthea Hucklesby, Kara Jarrold and Eleana Kazantzoglou. Robert Grice, David Ryan-Mills and Clair Wilkins assisted with data inputting and analysis. The team would like to thank the staff from the Effective Bail Scheme who assisted us with the collection of data and the individuals who gave up their time to be interviewed. We would also like to acknowledge the assistance we received from Ministry of Justice staff and staff at G4S in relation to electronically monitored curfew conditions

Introduction

The Effective Bail Scheme (EBS) operated in ten courts in Yorkshire and Humberside between 2006–10. It was originally funded from the Treasury Invest to Save Budget which funded innovative projects which forged partnerships to improve the quality and cost effectiveness of public services. It provided bail support for adult defendants to divert defendants from custodial remands, increase court attendance rates and compliance with bail conditions and reduce alleged offending on bail. The scheme provided accommodation and used volunteer mentors. The research relating to the process evaluation of the Effective Bail Scheme pilot was funded by the Ministry of Justice.[1]

Inevitably for a project of this kind which included an action research element, practices and procedures evolved and developed during the life time of the project. This report provides a snapshot of the scheme during the first 18 months of its operation between November 2006 and June 2008 after which the scheme moved on and developed further until it ended in June 2010. The purpose of this book is to provide a comprehensive picture of the operation of the EBS project in its first 18 months using quantitative and qualitative data. Before exploring the evaluation findings in detail in subsequent chapters, this chapter provides an overview of the prison remand population and bail law and practice with the aim of contextualising later discussions about the EBS and the provision of bail support more generally. After exploring some of the arguments for maximising the use of bail, the next section examines the prison remand population in order to explore the problem which the Effective Bail Scheme (and other bail support schemes) was aimed at alleviating. Following this, the chapter provides a brief overview of bail law and practice before turning its attention to current knowledge about bail support and bail information schemes.

Why bail?

According to the law in England and Wales and many other jurisdictions, defendants have a right to bail while they are awaiting trial. This is a fundamental human right based on the right to liberty and the presumption of innocence which is enshrined into the Human Rights Act 1998, the European Convention on Human Rights and the International Covenant on the Protection of Civil and Political Rights. The right to bail can be overturned by the courts if they believe that the risks posed by releasing defendants are too great. In these circumstances, defendants are remanded in custody to await their trial. In making a remand decision, courts have to weigh up a balance of probabilities. They have to balance the rights of defendants against the risks posed to victims, witnesses and the general public. In doing this, courts are required to assess defendants' future behaviour and because of this there are no certainties. In making their assessments, courts rely on information relating to defendants' past behaviour (offending and bail history) and their current circumstances, mainly in terms of their community ties (accommodation, employment, relationships and family situation). They also use assessments provided by the police and the Crown Prosecution Service.

There are a number of additional reasons why bail should never be refused unless there are significant grounds for doing so (Hucklesby, 2002). Defendants who are remanded in custody are housed in some of the worst conditions in the prison estate (HMIP, 2000). The additional rights which should be afforded to remand prisoners such as daily visits and wearing their own clothes often do not materialise in practice (HMIP, 2000). They are also held in local prisons where overcrowding is at its worst and the regimes at their most basic. Preparing for a court case is also more difficult from prison, access to legal advice is restricted which is a situation which is likely to have been worsened by recent cuts in legal aid and defendants are unable to search for evidence or witnesses themselves (HMIP, 2000). Custodial remands are also correlated with case outcomes with defendants who are remanded in custody being more likely to plead guilty, less likely to be acquitted and more likely to receive a custodial sentence although such correlations do not necessarily indicate causality (Ministry of Justice, 2010a). Being remanded in custody may have significant and long-lasting effects on defendants and their families. Defendants may lose their jobs or jeopardise future employment prospects. It may have considerable economic consequences which may result in the loss of the family home, and problems with the repayment of other loans. Emotional problems for both defendants and their families and friends may arise as well as the time and expense involved in relatives visiting defendants in prison.

There are serious consequences for individual defendants who are remanded in custody but the number of defendants remanded in custody also has an impact on the criminal justice system. These include most notably economic cost – the costs of keeping defendants in custody, the cost of escorting them between prisons and the courts and the cost of live-link facilities so that remand hearings can take place while defendants remain in prison. The most visible concern is the size of the prison remand population which has been a major driver in the search for alternatives to custodial remands. In the next section the prison remand population is examined.

The prison remand population in England and Wales

The prison population as a whole has been rising almost continuously since the end of the Second World War and particularly sharply since 1993. Between 1993 and 2009, the average prison population increased by 88% from 44,600 to 83,600 (Ministry of Justice, 2010b). By the summer of 2010 the prison population had reached 85,600 (Ministry of Justice, 2010c). Around 84% of the total were convicted and sentenced and this population has been the main driver of the increasing prison population in recent decades. For this reason, initiatives to reduce the prison population have often focused on the sentenced population including the introduction of measures such as Home Detention Curfew and the End of Custody Licence Scheme.

The remand population is a relatively small part of the prison population. In 2009 the annual average population of remand prisoners was 13,456 which accounts for 16% of the total population (Ministry of Justice, 2010b). This is in contrast to the 1980s when the increasing remand population was a significant driver of the rising prison population generally. As Morgan and Jones (1992) noted, 78% of the increase in the prison population (of 6390) between 1979 and 1989 was accounted for by the remand population. During the latter half of the 1980s and early 1990s the prison remand population made up over 20% of the total prison population reaching a high of 25% in 1994 (Home Office, 1993; Ministry of Justice, 2008a).

Figure 1.1 shows the annual average prison remand population between 1980 and 2009. It demonstrates that the prison remand population peaked at the end of the 1980s before temporarily dipping in the early 1990s before climbing once again until the end of the century. There was a respite in the early 2000s when the population fell before increasing in 2002 to around 13,000. Between 2002 and 2008 the prison remand population remained relatively stable at between 12,500 and 13,000 (Hucklesby, 2009).

Figure 1.1 Annual average prison remand population 1980–2009

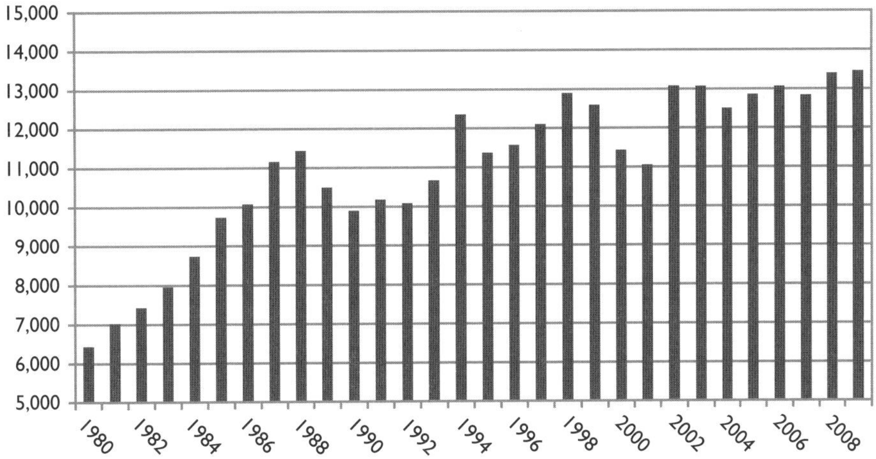

Source: Home Office, 1989; Ministry of Justice, 2008a, 2010b

The annual average remand population provides only a partial picture of the number of defendants who spend time in custody awaiting trial and does not allow for a consideration of fluctuations in the population during the year. The turnover of remand prisoners is much higher than in the sentenced population so many more individuals are incarcerated, albeit usually for less time. Figure 1.2 shows the number of remand prisoners received into prison between 2003 and 2009. It demonstrates that the number of receptions of remand prisoners has dropped from 91,188 in 2003 to 75,300 in 2009. The drop in the flow of remand prisoners into the prison estate is likely to have contributed to the stabilisation of the average number of prisoners held on remand since 2003 (see Hucklesby, 2009).

Figure 1.2 Receptions of remand prisoners 2003–09

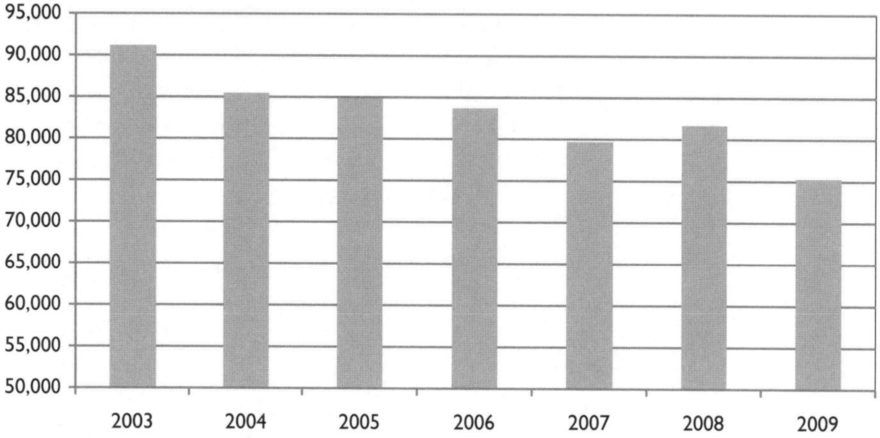

Source: Ministry of Justice, 2010b

The prison remand population comprises two groups of defendants: the untried and the convicted but unsentenced populations. The untried population comprises prisoners who are awaiting trial and are therefore unconvicted. They make up around two thirds of the prison remand population. The unsentenced population are prisoners who have been convicted and who are awaiting sentence. Figure 1.3 shows the annual average population of each of these groups. It demonstrates that the average number of untried remand prisoners has been increasing steadily since 2004 reaching a total of 8,933 in 2009. Contemporaneously, the average number of unsentenced prisoners has been falling reaching a total of 4,523 in 2009.

Figure 1.4 shows the number of receptions of untried and unsentenced prisoners between 2003 and 2009. It demonstrates that the number of unconvicted defendants entering prisons has remained relatively constant. Meanwhile, the number of unsentenced prisoners being remanded in custody has fallen steadily over the period. The Ministry of Justice (2010b) partly explains this trend by reference to the introduction of fast delivery reports. These reports provide decision-makers with details about defendants' backgrounds and the circumstances leading to offences more quickly than 'standard delivery reports' (pre-sentence reports as they were previously known) (National Probation Service, 2005a). Fast delivery reports have proved popular with those passing sentences with their use increasing each year since they were introduced (Ministry of Justice, 2010b). At the same time, the use of standard delivery reports has declined. Theoretically, fast delivery reports avoid

Figure 1.3 Annual average population of untried and unsentenced prisoners 2002–09

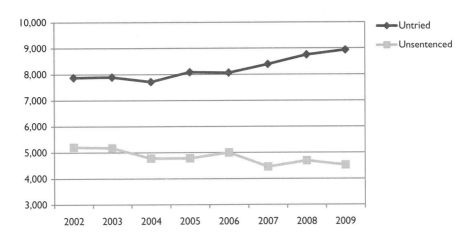

Source: Ministry of Justice, 2010b

the need to remand defendants because they should be produced on the same day as defendants are convicted (National Probation Service, 2005a, 2009a, 2009b). However, fast delivery reports should only be used in cases where offenders have committed less serious offences (National Probation Service, 2005a, 2009a, 2009b). This appears to be the practice with 84% of the reports written on defendants who are remanded in custody being standard delivery reports (Ministry of Justice, 2010b). Consequently, the introduction of fast delivery reports is unlikely to be a significant cause of the drop of more than a quarter in the number of receptions of unsentenced prisoners (Hucklesby, 2009).

It is possible that the introduction of the Community Order has had an impact on the number of defendants who are remanded in custody for sentencing. The Community Order introduced by the Criminal Justice Act 2003 replaced a range of community sentences with one order which can have up to 12 requirements. This might have simplified the decision-making process so that those passing sentence feel able to sentence offenders immediately rather than relying on reports which require a remand although no data are available to evaluate this supposition.

The number of remand prisoners entering prison is only part of the picture. The average number of remand prisoners is also affected by the length of time prisoners spend in prison. Indeed, the fact that the average number of untried prisoners has been increasing (see Figure 1.3) at the same time as the number of receptions of this group has been stable (see Figure 1.4) suggests that untried prisoners might be spending longer in prison awaiting trial. Unfortunately, data on the length of stay of remand prisoners is limited. The Ministry of Justice dropped the overall statistic from annual published data but the average time spent in custody by remand prisoners was 59 days in 2008 compared to 58 days in 2006 (Ministry of Justice, 2009a).

Figure 1.4 First receptions of untried and unsentenced prisoners 2003–09

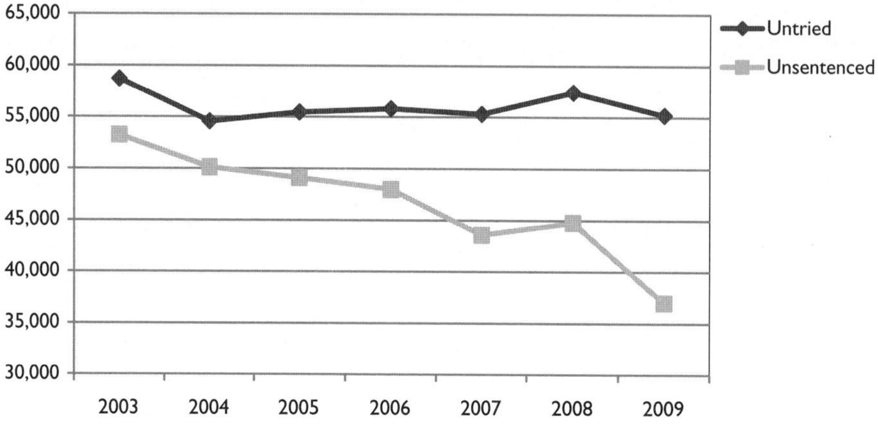

Source: Ministry of Justice, 2010b

The majority of the prison remand population are adult males (75%) (Ministry of Justice, 2010b). In 2009, 80% (10,832) of remand prisoners were adults and 94% (12,617) were males. Just under a third (30%, n=3981) of remand prisoners were from minority ethnic groups which is a slightly higher proportion than in the prison population as a whole which in turn is disproportionately high compared to their representation in the general population. Black prisoners constitute the largest single group of prisoners from minority ethnic groups (15%) compared with 8% Asian, 4% mixed race and 2% Chinese and other (Ministry of Justice, 2010b). The overrepresentation of prisoners from minority ethnic groups is concentrated in the male population where 30% of remand prisoners are from such groups (Ministry of Justice, 2010b). A quarter of the female remand population are from minority ethnic groups (Ministry of Justice, 2010b). These figures indicate that prisoners from minority ethnic groups, and particularly males, are overrepresented in the prison remand population suggesting that ethnicity may be a contributory factor in decisions to remand defendants in custody. Additionally, a slightly higher proportion of remand prisoners who declared a religion were Muslim (19%) compared with the same group in the sentence population (17%) suggesting that Muslim defendants may be overrepresented in the prison remand population when compared to their representation in the sentenced population (Ministry of Justice, 2010b). Official statistics do not allow the basis of the figures to be investigated so factors which may explain some of the differences between ethnic groups such as differences in offence types, bail and offending histories cannot be explored. It is an area in which further research is required to undercover whether discriminatory decision-making is taking place.

Prisoners charged with violence offences comprise the largest single group in the remand population and account for 26% of all remand prisoners. The next largest single offence category is drugs (14%) followed by robbery and burglary (both 11%) (Ministry of Justice, 2010b). Over the last decade the offences allegedly committed by remand prisoners have changed. In 1999, 18% of the remand population were charged with violence offences compared with a quarter in 2009 (Ministry of Justice, 2010b). Over the same period, the proportion of remand prisoners charged with burglary has decreased from a fifth (19%) to just over a tenth (11%) and for theft from 14% to 7% (Ministry of Justice, 2010b).

Having examined the prison remand population and some of its characteristics using official statistics, the next section provides an overview of the law and policy relating to bail.

Bail law, policy and practice

The main statue governing the grant of bail in England and Wales is the Bail Act 1976. The Act has been significantly amended since it became law in 1978. The Bail Act 1976 introduced a right to bail for all defendants and was introduced at a time when due process values were dominant. Research conducted in the late 1960s and 1970s had shown that defendants were being remanded in custody when they could be safely granted bail and the custodial remands had detrimental impacts on defendants and their cases (Bottomley, 1970; King, 1971). The general right to bail has since been significantly eroded by successive amendments to the legislation which have been introduced during a time when crime control concerns have been predominant and efforts have been made to reduce the time it takes for cases to be completed. Periodically, bail has become headline news usually as a result of specific cases either where serious offences were allegedly committed on bail (for example, when Winston Silcott was charged with the murder of PC Blakelock during the Broadwater farm riot in 1985) or where defendants allegedly committed numerous offences while on bail. The Association of Chief Police Officers (ACPO) were a driving force in seeking legislative change during the early 1990s when several police forces published in-house research relating to the extent of defendants offending while on bail. This research reportedly showed that nearly half of defendants released on bail offended (Avon and Somerset Constabulary, 1991; Greater Manchester Police, 1988; Northumbria Police, 1991). Events such as these have resulted in the spotlight falling on the bail process intermittently followed by calls for reform to ensure that certain categories of defendants are more easily remanded in custody.

The Bail Act 1976 (s.4) introduced a general right to bail, often termed a presumption in favour of bail, which requires the courts to release a person on bail unless certain conditions are met (outlined in Schedule 1 of the Act). The Bail Act 1976 (s.3.1) defines bail as the temporary release of an individual from court on condition that the individual surrenders to the custody of the court at a future date. Bail can be granted at several stages of the criminal justice process: while defendants are awaiting trial, when they have been convicted and are awaiting sentence and in the course of an appeal.

Legally, courts should always start from the premise that an individual has a right to bail and may only refuse bail if certain defined exceptions apply (Schedule 1 of the Bail Act 1976). The exceptions vary depending on whether or not the offence(s) with which the person is charged is imprisonable. In reality, however, most cases in which remand decisions are made relate to imprisonable offences. For these offences, there are three main exceptions to bail – risk of the defendant absconding, committing offences while on bail, or interfering with justice or obstructing justice. Under the original Bail Act (Schedule 1 Part 1, para 2) a defendant need not be granted bail if the court is satisfied that there are *substantial* grounds for believing that the defendant, if released on bail (with or without conditions), would: fail to surrender to custody; or commit an offence on bail; or interfere with witnesses or otherwise obstruct the course of justice, whether in relation to himself [sic] or any other person. Additionally a number of other exceptions can apply but are rarely used including that the courts have insufficient information to make a decision and for the defendant's own protection.

There is no specific definition of substantial grounds leaving decision-makers with considerable leeway. The Bail Act structures decision-makers' discretion by stating that courts should take account of range of factors including the offence, the background of the defendants, their previous bail history and the strength of the evidence. For defendants to be remanded in custody there needs to be evidence that the requirements of bail would not be met. For example, the grounds for refusing bail will be significantly strengthened if a defendant has a previous record of offending on bail or has committed the alleged offence while on bail.

The presumption in favour of bail has been significantly eroded since the Bail Act 1976 was enacted. Most of the amendments have been enacted in order to deal with the issue of offending on bail. Mirroring wider changes in sentencing law and policy, restrictions to the right to bail have dealt with defendants who have allegedly committed serious offences on bail (murder, manslaughter and rape, for example) and defendants who are believed to persistently commit offences while on bail. In terms of the first of these groups of defendants, the law requires courts to provide reasons *for* granting bail rather than for remanding defendants in custody in cases where serious offences have allegedly been committed. This requires courts to justify their decision to bail defendants, in effect overturning the presumption in favour of bail (Hucklesby, 2002).

Alleged offending on bail is an explicit exception to the right to bail. A series of legal changes culminated in the Criminal Justice Act 2003 which reverses the presumption of bail for defendants, who, it appears, are on bail at the time of the alleged offence, unless the court believes that there is no significant risk of offences being committed on bail. Theoretically, this should mean that defendants who are believed to have committed offences on bail whatever the seriousness are unlikely to be granted bail. However, decision-makers appear to require a certain threshold of seriousness before considering custodial remands so that defendants charged with less serious offences such as shoplifting are unlikely to be remanded in custody (Hucklesby, 2009). Also, the impact of the legislation is likely to have been minimal when dealing with serious offences. This is because it is unlikely that courts would have released defendants on bail who have been charged with a first, let alone a second, serious offence. As a result, this tightening up of the law on bail has been largely presentational in order to appease media and political concerns about offending on bail which generally have been based on sporadic and exceptional events (Hucklesby, 2009).

Although the courts decide issues of bail, its decisions are framed not only by the law but also by decisions earlier on in the remand process. Once a suspect has been charged with an offence, the police make a decision about whether to detain or bail defendants before the first court appearance. Their decision has an impact on court remand decisions (see Hucklesby, 1997a; Morgan and Henderson, 1998). If the police bail suspects, courts almost always bail them as well. The chances of a custodial remand are much greater if defendants were detained by the police (Hucklesby, 1996; Burrows et al, 1994; Morgan and Henderson, 1998). The police also influence court remand decisions through the recommendations they make to the Crown Prosecution Service (CPS). The relationship between police recommendations and subsequent CPS decisions about what representations to make to the court remains under-researched but one study found that there was a high level of agreement (Phillips and Brown, 1998). This arises partly because the CPS relies on the police file for information. In turn CPS representations greatly influence court remand decisions (Hucklesby, 1996). In light of these research findings which suggest that courts usually agree with CPS representations, it is surprising that parliament felt the need to give the CPS the right to appeal court decisions to grant bail in cases where they objected to bail (Bail (Amendment) Act 1993). To facilitate appeals, courts are required to give reasons for their decision to grant bail despite CPS objections (Criminal Justice and Police Act 2001). In essence this means that magistrates must justify their decision to grant bail in cases where the CPS obviously believes that the defendant should be remanded in custody. This is likely to make decision-makers think twice before bailing defendants when such circumstances apply and privileges CPS views above those of the court.

Any consideration of bail involves an assessment of risk in relation to future behaviour. Courts have to consider whether the person is likely to turn up for the trial, offend on bail or interfere with witnesses. There are no certainties, only predictions. These predictions are based on a range of factors including the nature and seriousness of the offence, previous record of offending, previous response(s) to bail, whether or not a custodial sentence is likely on conviction and the community ties of the defendant, especially whether or not they have a permanent home address (Morgan and Henderson, 1998; Doherty and East, 1985; Hucklesby, 1996). There is evidence to suggest that courts give greater weight to offence and offending-related factors than to community ties (Hucklesby, 1996). In making their decisions courts have to balance the risks which they can legally consider alongside more nebulous concerns about risks to the public against the requirements not to deprive legally innocent defendants of their liberty without good cause. The extent to which they get bail decisions right is open to question. In common with all forms of preventative detention, it is not possible to know how many of those who are detained would have complied with bail had they been released. Reliable data on the number of defendants who breach bail is also not available (Hucklesby, 2009). For example, we have no published data, only estimates, on the number of defendants who offend on bail and no agreed definition on what constitutes offending on bail (see Morgan, 1992; Hucklesby and Marshall, 2000). The amount of hidden offending on bail may be significant but we do not know. The information gap enables individuals or organisations to lobby for change on the basis of 'evidence' which cannot be substantiated.

One area where limited information is available is on the number of defendants who fail to attend court. Historically, ensuring that defendants turned up for trial was the principle purpose of bail (Bottomley, 1968; De Haas, 1940). While other considerations, namely preventing offending on bail, have risen in prominence, preventing absconding remains an important objective of the bail process (NAO, 2004). Defendants' non-attendance at court hearings has costs for the criminal justice process including wasted court time and the work involved in executing warrants. It also means that justice is delayed or denied with the result that victims may feel aggrieved. Around 15% of defendants are recorded as failing to appear each year (Ministry of Justice, 2010a) although official records are likely to be unreliable because of different court practices in dealing with non-attendance. Under the Bail Act 1976 failing to attend court hearings is a criminal offence.

Another measure of the reliability of bail decisions is the eventual outcome of cases. It can be argued that if defendants are found not guilty or are not given a custodial sentence then the decision to remand them in custody was wrong. However, this issue is complicated by the dynamic nature of cases during the pre-trial period which may mean that the facts of the cases change markedly and/or that plea bargaining occurs. Sentence discounts resulting from guilty pleas also impact on the eventual sentence. Morgan and Jones (1992) point out that those passing sentence may impose non-custodial sentences after custodial remands simply because they believe that offenders have already served sufficient time in custody. While the legitimacy of such an approach can be questioned, it means that the link between pre-trial decisions and sentencing decisions may not be as strong as might be supposed. Additionally, the risk of absconding, which is an important factor in bail decision-making, has little bearing on the case outcome potentially resulting in defendants being remanded in custody even though they are unlikely to receive a custodial sentence if convicted. In 2009, 13% of defendants who were remanded in custody were acquitted (Ministry of Justice, 2010a). Two-fifths of defendants who were remanded in custody did not serve a custodial sentence (Ministry of Justice, 2010a), including 16% who were given a community sentence or a suspended sentence and 7% who were given a fine or discharge (Ministry of Justice, 2010a).

Three-fifths (61%) of defendants who were remanded in custody were subsequently given a custodial sentence (National Statistics, 2010).The proportion of defendants receiving a custodial sentence having been remanded in custody has been rising in recent years. The coalition government has signalled its intention to increase this proportion further by ensuring that defendants who are not likely to receive a custodial sentence are not remanded in custody (Ministry of Justice, 2010d). How they intend to do this is unclear. Nevertheless a significant minority of defendants spend time in prison pre-trial but not after their cases have been dealt with. According to the Ministry of Justice, fewer women receive a custodial sentence after being remanded in custody than men, with 66% of women and 75% of men receiving an immediate custodial sentence (Ministry of Justice, 2010b).

This section provided a brief overview of the law on bail. In the next section, we turn our attention to data available from the Criminal Statistics (Ministry of Justice, 2010a) which relates to the courts' use of remand. It is not possible to make direct comparisons between the two sources of statistics on remand (Criminal Statistics and Prison Statistics) because of the way in which the statistics are compiled.

The use of bail

The proportion of remanded defendants who are remanded in custody has stayed relatively stable at around 10% since 2004 (Ministry of Justice, 2010a). In 2009, 61,000 defendants were remanded in custody representing 9% of the defendants who were remanded. Figure 1.5 shows that the number of defendants remanded in custody dropped steadily and consistently during the early years of the 21st century from 98,000 in 1999 to 52,000 in 2007. The figures have risen in 2008 and 2009 yet it is unclear whether these increases are real or a result of more accurate recording of data due to different data collection mechanisms (Ministry of Justice, 2010a). Particularly apparent from Figure 1.5 is the large increase in the number of defendants bailed by the courts in 2009 when compared with previous years. Again this may not be a real increase but might worryingly suggest that the number of individuals caught up in the remand process has been significantly underestimated for many years. Whatever the explanation, it means that nearly 600,000 defendants were on bail at some time during 2009. This figure alone suggests that we need to know much more about what restrictions defendants might be under and the experiences of defendants who are granted bail.

Official data suggest that Black defendants are significantly more likely to be remanded in custody than defendants from other ethnic groups. In 2009, nearly half of all black defendants dealt with at a Crown Court were remanded in custody compared with around a third of white defendants and defendants from other ethnic backgrounds (Ministry of Justice, 2010a). The differences persist for nearly all offence types and data are not available to investigate other explanations such as differences in offending and bail histories (Ministry of Justice, 2010a). In the absence of data it is impossible to understand why these differences exist, raising suspicions that discrimination is occurring in remand decisions. This view is supported by a number of research studies which have demonstrated that real differences exist in remand decisions for defendants from minority ethnic groups (for example, see Brown and Hullin, 1993).

Figure 1.5 Number of defendants remanded on bail and in custody 1999–2009

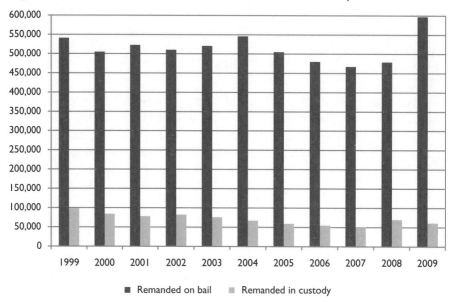

Source: Ministry of Justice, 2010a

Women are less likely than men to be remanded in custody (Ministry of Justice 2010e). In 2009, 20% of women and 38% of men dealt with at a Crown Court where remanded in custody. Given that women generally commit less serious offences than men, have shorter and less serious offending histories (see Ministry of Justice, 2010e) this is what would be expected, although published data is extremely limited, which makes it hard to investigate the issue any further in terms of why this might be the case.

Conditional bail

Bail can be granted unconditional or conditional. A person on unconditional bail is required to turn up for their next court hearing and not to offend. The term unconditional bail is unfortunate as this type of bail does place defendants on a duty to the court in terms of having to appear for the next court hearing. Also, being on bail is treated seriously by the court and is seen as an aggravating factor if any further offending takes place.

Bail conditions were introduced by the Criminal Justice Act 1967 and were later enshrined in the Bail Act 1976. They were primarily introduced as a mechanism to divert defendants from custody although they have additional functions including providing reassurance to courts, operating as risk management tools and enabling decision-makers to defend their decisions if problems arise (Hucklesby, 2009). Conditions perform these functions because they explicitly acknowledge that bail risks were known to the court when bail was granted. There is little doubt that the rise of a risk adverse culture in criminal justice has contributed to the increase in the use of conditions although statistical evidence of this trend from official sources is not available.

In order for conditions to be applied to bail courts must find that they are necessary to ensure that defendants: surrender to custody; do not commit an offence on bail; do not interfere with witnesses or otherwise obstruct the course of justice; and make themselves available for reports to be prepared. If conditions of bail are breached the defendant can be arrested (s.7 of the Bail Act 1976) and brought back to court for bail to be reconsidered. Breaching conditions is not a criminal offence.

Courts have wide discretionary powers to attach to bail whatever conditions they believe are necessary to deal with bail risks. In practice, they utilise a narrow range of conditions including residence requirements, curfews, exclusion zones, no contact conditions and reporting to the police station (Hucklesby, 1994a; Raine and Willson, 1994, 1996). Significant questions arise about the effectiveness, usefulness and enforceability of bail conditions as well as the decisions which courts take when defendants appear having breached bail conditions (Hucklesby, 1994a; Hucklesby, 2001; Raine and Willson, 1994, 1996). Sureties and securities, requiring the deposit of virtual and actual money respectively as a precondition to defendants being released, are not widely used by the courts in England and Wales. By contrast, sureties are the main form of release in the US leading to concerns about discrimination against defendants with few or no economic resources.

No information on the use of conditional bail is published officially. Consequently it is not known how many defendants are subject to bail conditions or the types of conditions by which they are required to abide. This information is available only from research studies. These studies suggest that conditional bail is now the norm rather than the exception with the latest findings suggesting that over half of the defendants who are bailed are required to abide by conditions (Airs et al, 2000; Hucklesby et al, 2007). Little attention has been paid to conditions of bail, but given that they may impose considerable restrictions on defendants' liberty their overuse and/or misuse should raise serious concerns. Bail conditions provide a mechanism to control and monitor defendants who are legally innocent and for this reason alone further research is required into how they are used and enforced and whether they increase compliance with bail.

Several new conditions have been made available to the courts in recent years including electronically monitored curfew orders, Restriction on Bail and bail support schemes. These recently introduced conditions will be discussed below. The bail conditions were introduced primarily as alternatives to custodial remands although this was not always explicitly acknowledged by the governments who implemented them. They provide additional safeguards to increase the confidence of the courts that any risks that defendants pose are minimised making the granting of bail more likely. Little research has been done specifically on whether bail conditions successfully divert defendants from custody but parallels can be drawn with the literature relating to community sentences. In relation to electronic monitoring, two studies have found that it diverts offenders from custody in about 50% of cases in which it is imposed (Lobley and Smith, 2000; Mair and Mortimer, 1996). This is consistent with the more general literature on community sentences which suggests that measures introduced as alternatives to custody work in this way in no more than half of cases (see Mair, 2009). Consequently, it seems likely that significant net-widening has occurred with defendants who would have received bail with less stringent conditions or no conditions having additional conditions attached to their bail.

Electronically monitored curfew conditions were introduced as a pilot in the 1980s but met with little success (Mair and Nee, 1990). They were introduced on a permanent basis in September 2005. Curfews have always been popular bail conditions but concerns existed about their enforceability and the impact that physically checking up on defendants had on police workloads (see Hucklesby, 1994a; Raine and Willson, 1994, 1996). Electronic monitoring assisted with both of these problems increasing courts' confidence in curfews. Electronically monitored curfews are used quite extensively and increasingly in the remand process. In March 2010, around 5,500 defendants were subject to electronically monitored bail conditions with just under 3,500 new starts in that month (Ministry of Justice, 2010f). This can be compared to March 2009 when 3,500 defendants were subject to such curfews (Ministry of Justice, 2009c). Whether the introduction of electronic monitoring has diverted defendants from custody is debatable. One study suggested that about half of the defendants subject to electronically monitored curfew conditions would have been remanded in custody while the remainder would have been granted bail in any event (Airs at al, 2000). In Scotland, where the system operates with specific safeguards to prevent net-widening, Barry et al (2007) found that electronic monitoring was being used as an alternative to custodial remands. The Labour government signalled its intention that electronically monitored curfew conditions were alternatives to custody because they introduced a time served credit for any subsequent prison sentence (Ministry of Justice, 2008b). Defendants are credited for half a day's imprisonment for every curfew period of nine hours or greater. This explicitly acknowledges the restriction of liberty involved in curfew orders but might also increase the use of short prison sentences on conviction as a way of explicitly recognising the time defendants spend remanded in custody. The downside is that it might put defendants at greater risk of a custodial remand and/or an immediate prison sentence if they are charged with an offence at a later date.

A second recently introduced bail condition is Restriction on Bail (RoB). A major driver of criminal justice policy in recent years has been the desire to tackle the problem of drug related offending. Policies have been implemented throughout the criminal justice process with the aim of channelling drug users into treatment (see Hucklesby and Wincup, 2010). By 2000, evidence of defendants misusing drugs could be considered when determining bail (The Criminal Justice and Court Services Act 2000). Following on from this, RoB was introduced by the Criminal Justice Act 2003 and subsequently amended by the Drugs Act 2005 (see Hucklesby, 2010). These Acts amended the Bail Act 1976 to enable RoB to be imposed by the courts. For RoB to be applied defendants must be over 18 and have tested positive for a specified Class A drug. Courts must be also be 'satisfied that there are substantial grounds for believing that the offences were caused, wholly or partly, by defendants' misuse of specified Class A drugs or were motivated, wholly or partly, by drug use to impose RoB. RoB is a condition of bail which requires defendants to undergo drug assessment and treatment as directed (see Hucklesby et al, 2007). If defendants refuse to attend assessments and/or participate in any relevant follow up (treatment or other support) they must be denied bail unless the court is satisfied that there is no significant risk of offences being committed on bail. Thus, the presumption of bail is reversed in such situations. This part of RoB was strengthened by the Drugs Act 2005. Originally, the Criminal Justice Act 2003 provided more discretion to the courts when considering what to do if defendants refused to comply with RoB by using the legal wording 'shall' rather than 'must' remand them in custody. Subsequently, the Drugs Act 2005 took away nearly all of the courts' discretion but retained just enough to stymie any potential legal challenges on the basis of a breach of the Human Rights Act 1998 (see Hucklesby, 2010). RoB has channelled defendants who are drug users into treatment but evidence of long-term impacts on offending or drug use is not available (Hucklesby et al, 2007). Its introduction also raises questions about the whether it is ethical to coerce legally innocent individuals into drug treatment (see Hucklesby, 2010).

A third bail condition is the requirement for defendants to attend a bail support scheme. Bail support schemes have been in existence since at least the late 1980s so they are not new. They draw on traditional models of welfare orientated probation practices (Drakeford et al, 2001). Traditionally they have been aimed at juveniles and youths rather than adults. Youth Offending Services have a statutory requirement to provide such services under the Crime and Disorder Act 1998 (see Thomas and Hucklesby, 2002). Ring-fenced funding was initially provided for this purpose but ceased subsequently requiring Youth Offending Services to provide bail support services through core budgets and resources. Bail support services for adults are far less common and there has been no national requirement for such services to be provided until recently.

The idea behind bail support services is similar for adults and youths and can be defined as:

> the provision of services (intervention and support) designed to help defendants awaiting trial or sentence to successfully complete their periods on bail within the

community by providing support and services matched to their circumstances, the alleged offence and the grounds for refusal of bail. (Thomas and Hucklesby, 2002: 40)

In practice, bail support schemes vary considerably mainly because they have traditionally been local initiatives. Cavadino and Gibson (1993) describe how schemes usually include one or more of the following elements: reporting requirements, agreed levels of contact with bail support workers and/or mentors, residence requirements and/or accommodation provision, assistance with a range of needs including employment, finances, education and family issues including referral to other agencies and programmes of activities to make constructive use of leisure time and to develop community ties. The wide range of commitments and services which may be encompassed by bail support schemes makes defining them tricky. It also raises questions about what they should be doing given defendants' unconvicted status. Theoretically this status should preclude working on factors associated with alleged offending behaviour and more especially the alleged offence for which defendants are on bail. Yet the distinction between providing support and criminogenic needs is likely to be blurred in practice making the division difficult to make. Arguably the distinction has already become blurred in law with the introduction of required assessment at the police station and RoB, both of which mandate identified drug users charged with offences to undergo drug treatment. These measures have significantly eroded the notion that unconvicted defendants should not be required to engage with services provided to deal with factors associated with their alleged offending because they are presumed to be innocent.

Historically some bail support schemes have been run on a voluntary basis. More recently they also operate as a requirement of the court whereby bail support is imposed as an explicit condition of bail. In these circumstances, non-compliance with bail support is dealt with as a breach of bail conditions with the threat of a custodial remand being imposed. Theoretically, bail support schemes are aimed at defendants at risk of being remanded in custody essentially operating as an alternative to custodial remands. Ashworth (1992) describes them as a 'middle path' between remands on conditional bail and in custody. Bail support schemes provide courts with some confidence that defendants will be monitored and their needs addressed while on bail thus enabling them to bail defendants whom they would otherwise perceive as 'too risky'.

The aims of bail support schemes are generally to reduce custodial remands, increase court attendance and reduce levels of offending on bail. They, therefore, address two of the main objections to bail under the Bail Act 1976 namely the risk of absconding and offending on bail, and potentially a third – interference with witnesses. Supplementing bail support with accommodation provision, which is linked most strongly to the risk of non-attendance at court, theoretically enables bail support schemes to have an impact on all of the principal reasons why bail may be refused legally.

As with all measures to divert defendants/offenders from custody, net-widening is a danger. While there is insufficient evidence to draw valid conclusions about the extent of net-widening from bail support schemes it might be assumed, on the basis of evidence relating to the use of community sentences reviewed above, that up to half of defendants bailed onto bail support schemes would have been bailed in any event (Mair, 2009). Considering ways to reduce net-widening effects is an important consideration for bail support schemes.

Until the creation of the Bail Accommodation and Support Service in 2007 (of which more later) there has never been national coverage of bail support provision for adults. Instead, local schemes have been set up on a largely ad hoc basis when funding has been available. During the early 1990s, when bail services were funded by the Home Office and operated by Probation Services, several bail support schemes for adults were introduced (Cavadino and Gibson, 1993; Drakeford et al, 2001). While there is little robust evidence of their effectiveness, studies suggest that they were cheaper than remanding defendants in custody and diverted some defendants from custodial remands without significant levels of non-compliance or breach (see Drakeford et al, 2001). However, evidence is thin on the ground and many of the schemes closed because of lack of funding before they could be fully evaluated (see Drakeford et al, 2001). An evaluation of a scheme for juveniles in Northern Ireland (NIO, 2006) suggested that it was viewed as a positive development by many and uncovered some evidence that it could have a positive impact on offending and breaches. The report concluded that, at the very least, bail support schemes offer defendants support and help to maximise the likelihood that they will abide by their bail conditions (NIO, 2006). In sum, there is a view that bail support schemes should work in theory but little evidence of their effectiveness exists, particularly in relation to adults.

Remand services have always been a 'Cinderella' service for statutory agencies who concentrate their efforts and resources on offenders who have been convicted rather than defendants awaiting trial. The Probation Service has been at best ambivalent towards providing remand services and at worst objected to it (Drakeford et al, 2001; Haines and Octigan, 1999) partly because probation staff did not view pre-trial services as their responsibility and partly because they believed that resources should be used for their core work with offenders. Voluntary sector providers have often filled this gap. Prior to the Crime and Disorder Act 1998, bail support services within youth justice were frequently provided by voluntary sector organisations who have a long tradition of providing add-on services within criminal justice (Carey and Walker, 2002). The current policy agenda of the National Offender Management Service clearly identifies a move towards the voluntary and private sectors increasingly becoming providers of criminal justice services (Carter, 2003). Bail support services for adults have in recent years been provided by the voluntary and private sectors. This is not unexpected given current agendas and the fact that the remand process is often used as a testing ground for new initiatives (for example, the introduction of prison sector prisons (see James et al, 1997), and electronic monitoring (Mair and Nee, 1990)) and the ambivalence of the Probation Service to involvement in bail services. The Effective Bail Scheme (EBS), which is the focus of this publication, was originally a multi-sector initiative which tested out the ability of voluntary sector organisations to work together and alongside statutory agencies to provide a bail support service to the criminal justice system. This set-up was one of the innovative features of the scheme, which enabled a successful bid to be made to the Treasury under the Invest to Save Budget.

While the EBS was running, the National Offender Management Service (NOMS) set up a second bail support scheme aimed at adults – the Bail Accommodation and Support Service (BASS) (Ministry of Justice, 2007). The scheme began in June 2007 and was created in response to an apparent shortage of suitable bail accommodation which partly arose because of the almost exclusive use of approved premises for high-risk offenders (National Probation Service, 2008; Burnett and Eaton, 2004). The aim of BASS is to reduce the number of defendants remanded in custody. It provides accommodation and support for defendants bailed by the courts. Under the original contract defendants received three one-hour support sessions for the first three weeks on the scheme which reduced to one session a week thereafter. In line with the EBS, support-only packages were available for defendants who already had suitable bail accommodation.

BASS is a national service which was originally operated by a private company, ClearSprings Management Limited. From June 2010, Stonham, the UK largest housing association, has been running the scheme (www.stonham-bass.org.uk/frmHomepage.aspx; NOMS, 2010). The scheme provides accommodation in small units in the community. The fact that the houses were located in residential areas resulted in a storm of criticism when ClearSprings were operating the scheme relating predominantly to claims that bail hostels were being set up without the requisite planning permission or the knowledge of local councils (see, for example, Doward, 2008; Kirkup, 2008). These concerns were partially dealt with by a protocol between ClearSprings and the Local Government Association which provided for consultation before accommodation was set up (Local Government Association, 2009) although questions continued to be asked in parliament about the scheme (see Hansard, 2010). BASS has also had a difficult implementation more generally. At least some of the concerns voiced about BASS arose because of the great speed at which the service was set up. This resulted in poor consultation with other agencies such as the Probation Service and the necessary infrastructure was not in place so that large parts of the country had no accommodation available. These problems were compounded by delays in the assessment process. Take-up was low with 1,385 defendants being bailed to the scheme up to January 2009 (Hansard, 2009a, 2009b). Structural issues also existed with the service. It explicitly dealt with low-risk defendants so the extent to which it diverted defendants from custody was questionable. Any defendants with a conviction for a sexual offence, however long ago and/or minor were excluded from the scheme. In terms of the EBS, BASS represented an alternative model of service provision. To avoid overlap BASS did not operate in the courts in which the EBS operated but confusion among court staff and defence solicitors about which scheme to approach arose particularly in prison bail information schemes where demarcations made in relation to which court was covered by which scheme was less clear. BASS is now operating in all areas with the EBS being subsumed into it in June 2010.

Bail information schemes

Bail information schemes date back to the 1970s when they were introduced to increase the quantity and quality of information available to courts in order for them to make more accurate bail decisions. They were based on the Manhattan Bail Project which focused on providing verified information to courts in order to increase the likelihood that defendants would be granted bail (Ares et al, 1963). They were first proposed in the UK in 1974 (Home Office, 1974) and soon after this, the first court-based scheme was established in Inner London (ILPAS, 1976). As well as providing bail information, this scheme offered bail support with involved intensive social work. The scheme was viewed as successful as it increased the number of defendants granted bail and the bail support element was seen as crucial to this (Lloyd, 1992). Despite this promising conclusion, the idea of bail information schemes lay dormant until 1986 when the Association of Chief Officers of Probation (ACOP) set up eight schemes with Home Office funding. The aim of these schemes was to provide the Crown Prosecution Service with verified, factual and favourable information about defendants' community ties (housing, employment, dependants and so on), which was relevant to the issue of bail. The information provided would aid the newly created Crown Prosecution Service to make informed decisions because the information provided through the bail information scheme would counter-balance information the CPS received from the police. As a consequence, the CPS might be more likely to override police objections to bail. The explicit intention of the schemes was to reduce the number of defendants in custody. Unlike the previous pilot, the schemes simply provided information and were not involved in bail support.

The schemes were successful as at least some defendants were granted bail who would otherwise have been remanded in custody and they were cost effective (Lloyd, 1992; Mair, 1988; Stone, 1988). As a result, bail information schemes were extended nationally. These schemes provided factual, verified information about defendants to the CPS and a copy was also provided to the defence solicitor. Only positive information was included in bail information reports because of the stated aim of the scheme was to decrease the number of unnecessary custodial remands. By 1993, 179 court-based bail information schemes covering 35 probation areas were operational. The research into these schemes suggested that they successfully diverted defendants from custodial remands in several ways, by affecting CPS decisions to object to bail and defence decisions to apply for bail and by strengthening bail applications by the defence (Godson and Mitchell, 1991; Hucklesby, 1994b; Lloyd, 1992; Warner and McIvor, 1994). For example, Godson and Mitchell (1991) found that the CPS rejected 27% of police recommendations for custodial remands when bail information was not provided compared to 49% when it was. Schemes were particularly successful for homeless defendants (Lloyd, 1992). Bail information schemes have always been linked strongly to finding accommodation for defendants who otherwise would not have a bail address and were viewed by some criminal justice professionals as purely an accommodation service (Hucklesby, 1994b). Bail accommodation has always proved difficult to source even when bail hostels were available (Hucklesby, 1994b). The very important factor in the success of bail information schemes in the 1990s, in terms of reducing the number of defendants remanded in custody, was that the reports were prepared primarily for the CPS but also provided to defence solicitors and not the court. This was a departure from the American schemes but given that 98% of remand decisions in magistrates' courts coincide with CPS recommendations it was a key factor in their success (Hucklesby, 1996). Hucklesby (1994b) also found that bail information schemes were valued because they saved court time and provided independent information.

The provision of court-based bail information schemes began to decline in the mid-1990s when ring-fenced funding was withdrawn and other probation tasks took priority. At this time, the Probation Service had no statutory duty to provide bail information reports. Nevertheless, in 1999, the provision of bail information became a key performance indicator for the Probation Service although it related to CPS satisfaction with the provision of bail information rather than targets for its coverage (Home Office, 2000). By 2000, the Labour government, as part of its comprehensive spending review, had decided that bail information was cost efficient and required probation services to provide bail information in all magistrates' courts (Home Office, 2000). No additional resources were forthcoming and the expectation was that court teams would provide bail information alongside other tasks except in courts where workloads required specific posts to be created. The purpose of bail information also changed as a result of the Probation Circular PC29/2000 (Home Office, 2000). While it was acknowledged that bail information could reduce remands in custody, the focus was on providing information to courts in order to improve the accuracy of its decision-making. To this end, bail information was required to provide both positive and negative information about defendants (Home Office, 2000). In this way, bail information's role as a source of independent verified information about defendants would be enhanced. The primary recipient of reports was still the CPS with copies also being given to defence solicitors and probation court duty staff.

Despite government attempts to increase the availability of bail information by 2003 the number of bail information reports prepared in England and Wales as a whole had decreased from around 25,000 in 1996 to below 10,000 in 2003 (NAO, 2004). National Probation Service statistics confirmed this trend finding that the number of reports had declined from a peak of around 25,000 reports in 1997 to under 6,000 in 2003 (NPS), 2005b). The provision of bail information was concentrated into certain areas with only around 55% of magistrates' courts covered by bail information schemes and in some areas no reports were being prepared (NPS, 2005b). These events could have been predicted given the findings of a Probation Inspectorate report (HMIPro, 1993: 15) which concluded that bail services were often 'marginalised', received 'insufficient management attention' and that 'some parts of the Probation Service have been unsure of the professional value of such work'. These attitudes were confirmed when the provision of bail information was not prioritised (NPS, 2005b). In short, bail information schemes were not viewed as core business for the Probation Service and some viewed such schemes as outside the remit of the service (see for example, Fiddes, 1989). This view was supported by the assessment of bail information as of 'medium' priority to the Probation Service by the Probation Priority Framework Guidance in 2002 (Home Office, 2005). Over the same period, the provision of bail hostel places declined as a result of the realignment of hostels as a resource primarily for high-risk offenders serving community sentences or being released from prison. The impact of this on bail information was that they were left with no accommodation provision to offer courts which had been an important element in their success in the early 1990s (Hucklesby, 1994b).

One of the main impetuses for the resurrection of bail information schemes in the early part of the 21st century was the National Audit Office (2004) report on non-appearance of bailed defendants. This report suggested that bail information schemes had a role to play in reducing non-appearances at court hearings by defendants on bail as well as providing credible information to the court and reducing the number of defendants remanded in custody (NAO, 2004). It suggested that the National Offender Management Service (NOMS) should assess the costs and benefits of bail information schemes. Consequently, the National Probation Service (2005b: 3) asked probation areas to 'reassess current bail information procedures' and identify how bail information reports could be provided for some groups of defendants, namely women, the young, defendants from minority ethnic groups, vulnerable defendants, prolific and priority offenders and those likely to cause harm, reoffend or fail to attend court.

A pilot bail information scheme was set up in Yorkshire and Humberside in 2006 funded from the national Pathfinder Initiative (Harris and Robinson, 2008). The scheme ran alongside the Effective Bail Scheme and was the gatekeeper to the bail support scheme. The aim of the pilot was to assess the operation of bail information schemes in six courts (Bradford, Hull, Leeds, Scarborough, Sheffield and York). This scheme differed from previous schemes in that the primary target for reports were magistrates and District Judges although reports were also given to the CPS and defence solicitors. The in-house evaluation of the scheme (Harris and Robinson, 2008) suggested that it diverted defendants from custody but only when bail support operated alongside it and that some stakeholders did not view bail information as a useful standalone service. However, magistrates and CPS staff suggested that bail information saved time and provided valuable objective information. There was some indication that the scheme struggled to provide an effective service in larger courts because of a lack of resources and that this had an impact on the number of defendants diverted from custody (Harris and Robinson, 2008).

Bail information schemes are integral to bail support services because they identify potential defendants for the schemes. Consequently, added impetus for the (re) establishment of the bail information scheme nationally was provided by the setting up of BASS. Bail support schemes rely on bail information schemes to identify potential defendants for their schemes and assess their suitability. In the case of the EBS, probation areas provided bail information, identifying eligible defendants, assessing them and preparing a report to the court indicating whether defendants were suitable for bail support. While the process was similar for BASS when ClearSprings was operating the scheme, a second assessment was carried out by the service provider to assess suitability, whereas the EBS relied almost exclusively on probation assessments. The relationship between probation and the agencies operating bail support services is, therefore, critical to the success of bail support schemes. Bail information schemes and bail support schemes running alongside each other make it difficult to unpack the impact of each scheme on bail decisions. It raises questions about the extent to which each scheme contributes to any reduction in custodial remands, whether the schemes are mutually reinforcing and the value added by each scheme.

This chapter has reviewed available evidence relating to the prison remand population, the use of bail in England and Wales, the options available to courts and the genesis and operation of bail support and bail information schemes. The following chapters examine the findings of the evaluation of the EBS. Chapter Two describes the research design of the evaluation. Chapter Three introduces the EBS and examines its governance and staffing structures. Chapter Four assesses the take-up and caseload of the EBS and explores the characteristics of the defendants on the EBS and in some cases compares them to defendants who were remanded in custody. Chapter Five examines the work undertaken by the EBS with defendants. Chapter Six analyses stakeholders' and defendants' views of the EBS gleaned from interviews. Chapter Seven considers interim outcome measures and Chapter Eight highlights the main conclusions of the report and discusses potential future developments.

Note

[1] A summary of the findings of the evaluation can be found at www.justice.gov.uk/ effective-bail-scheme-monitoring.htm

Evaluation design and methodology

2

This chapter provides details of the design of the evaluation and methodology employed. It examines the aims and objectives of the evaluation before providing details of the ways in which data were gathered.

Aims and objectives of the evaluation

The overall aim of the evaluation was to assess the impact of the Effective Bail Scheme (EBS) together with the Bail Information Pathfinder (BIP) on custodial remands, court attendance rates, compliance with bail conditions, offending on bail and the provision of low risk accommodation, as well as to assess the costs and benefits of the bail schemes particularly in terms of prison places. The evaluation aimed, also, to examine partnership working between NOMS and the voluntary sector and to identify effective practice in relation to the provision of bail schemes. The evaluation was funded and overseen by the Ministry of Justice.

The evaluation was an implementation and process evaluation which had the primary aim of improving the operation of the bail schemes and took the form of action research. In addition, monitoring data were collected to assess the interim outcomes of the scheme. The original intention was to include an outcome and economic evaluation but this was deemed not to be viable by the funders. The more specific objectives were to:

* examine the implementation process for EBS;
* identify effective practice in terms of implementing EBS;
* identify the role of BIP in the EBS process;
* describe the BIP and EBS process and produce process maps;
* examine the operation of EBS and BIP (where applicable) including assessment and referral mechanisms and the provision of bail support;
* identify similarities and differences in the operation of BIP and EBS in different courts;
* identify barriers to the effective implementation and/or operation of EBS and BIP (where applicable);
* identify and examine the effectiveness of the breach procedures;
* identify and examine breach outcomes;
* assess the early take up of EBS and accommodation provision;
* identify and examine the components of EBS packages;
* explore the role of mentors in EBS;
* investigate the role and impact of accommodation provision to EBS;

- assess early indicators of the effectiveness of EBS including compliance rates with EBS and other bail conditions and court attendance rates;
- identify and examine sentencing outcomes for defendants on the EBS;
- investigate how EBS operates alongside other criminal justice interventions such as Restriction on Bail (RoB), Drug Intervention Programme (DIP) and community orders;
- assess levels and effectiveness of staff training and supervision;
- investigate workers and stakeholders views and experiences of EBS;
- investigate defendants' views and experiences of EBS including levels of compliance and offending.
- assess the extent and effectiveness of partnership working and identify any barriers to it; and
- investigate workers', managers' and other stakeholders' views of partnership working.

Research design

The evaluation was a process evaluation which used multiple methodologies to collect data. These included: observations, the collection and analysis of administrative data, and interviews with workers, stakeholders and defendants. Each of the methodologies will be discussed in turn below.

Observations

A range of observational activities were undertaken to enable process maps to be completed, an in-depth knowledge and understanding of the operation of the EBS to be obtained, and to identify effective practice and any barriers to it. Observations included the BIP and EBS processes, the work of the BIP and EBS workers and mentors, the EBS management team, court remand hearings and Partnership Board and project meetings.

Administrative data

Administrative data were collated from bail information records, case files of defendants who had been on the EBS, 544 mentoring files collated by SOVA and records kept by Foundation Housing relating to accommodation. Together these data provided information on defendants' backgrounds including offending and bail histories, details of the case, court decisions, the work undertaken by the EBS and defendants' compliance.

Data were collated mainly from paper files kept by bail information and bail support staff. A database providing basic information was kept by bail information staff but no electronic records were kept by the EBS until August 2008 when a database providing details of all cases dealt with by the EBS was completed retrospectively. The quality of the data from all sources was patchy. Data were missing or misrecorded. For example, some areas kept previous conviction records for all defendants assessed by bail information staff while other areas destroyed these when defendants were not bailed to the scheme. Data were also recorded differently between and within areas leading to inconsistencies as well as gaps in available data. The research team were able to plug gaps in data through triangulation of data sources but some data remained missing.

Interviews

A total of 196 semi-structured interviews were undertaken with a range of individuals including all except one of the personnel involved in the management and operation of the scheme. Wherever possible, project staff who left before the end of the project were interviewed. Interviews lasted between one and three hours. Most of the interviews took place between February and May 2008. Table 2.1 provides details of the interviewees and when they were interviewed.

Remand decision-makers, legal advisors, CPS lawyers and Associate Prosecutors were interviewed in each of the courts (the breakdown by area is presented in Table 2.2). These interviews took place between November and April 2008. Unfortunately, major difficulties were encountered in finding defence solicitors who would agree to be interviewed. Consequently, numbers are particularly low in some of the court areas. A total of 21 mentors were interviewed between October 2007 and May 2008. This included all of the mentors who were active during the period when the interviews were taking place. Interviews with these groups lasted between 30 minutes and an hour and a half.

A total of 44 defendants were interviewed between October 2007 and May 2008. Table 2.2 shows that they were spread fairly evenly between the areas with slightly more interviews being conducted in Bradford, Hull, Leeds and Sheffield than in Scarborough and York. The majority of the interviewees were male (n=35) and described their ethnic origin as white British (n=35). The mean age was 29. The ages ranged from 19 and 44 years. The sample is broadly representative of the defendants who have been subject to bail support. Interviewees were given £15 in High Street vouchers for agreeing to be interviewed. No defendants refused to be interviewed.

The content of the interviews varied considerably depending on individuals' involvement with the scheme. Senior managers and stakeholders were asked about their involvement in the scheme, their understanding of the scheme and its role; the role of the Ministry of Justice, National Offender Management Service, Regional Offender Manager's Office and the Probation areas; operational issues, bail information, bail support, housing, mentoring, breach, partnership working, project management, accountability structures; funding and financial issues, effectiveness,

Table 2.1 Interviewees

	Number	Timing
Senior management/Partnership interviews		
Nacro management	3	May 08
MoJ	1	April 08
Yorkshire and Humberside ROMs office	2	May–June 08
SOVA	1	May 08
Foundation Housing	2	May 08
HMCS representative	1	May 08
Probation representative	1	May 08
Police	5	June 08
G4S	3	May 08
Courts		
District judges	7	Feb–May 08
Magistrates	32	Feb–May 08
Legal advisors	14	Feb–May 08
CPS	15	Oct 07–March 08
Defence solicitors	10	Dec 07–April 08
Probation areas		
Assistant chief officers	4	May 08
Senior probation officers (court teams)	6	May 08
Project staff		
Senior staff	8	Nov 07–May 08
Workers	19	May 08
Mentors	21	Oct 07–May 08
Defendants	44	Oct 07–May 08
Total	**198**	

comparisons with the Bail Accommodation and Support Scheme (BASS) and the future of the EBS.

Interviews with EBS staff took place in May 2008. They were asked about their background and their post, training and supervision, the role of EBS, operational issues, project management, relationships with colleagues and RoB team, working with criminal justice professionals, partnership issues, working with defendants, reflections on practice, housing, mentoring, breach, sentencing, BASS and the future of the EBS.

Criminal Justice professionals were asked about their role, training and information they had received about the project, the role and operation of the bail information scheme and the EBS, impact of remand decision-making, compliance and breach, alleged offending on EBS, sentencing, outcomes and the future of EBS.

Defendants were asked for demographic and background information including their housing status, bail and offending history. These interviews also asked about defendants' knowledge and expectations of the scheme, the EBS process, the bail information interview, the nature and content of contacts with the EBS, the work undertaken with them, perceptions of workers, the usefulness of the work undertaken and its impact particularly on compliance and offending, mentoring and accommodation and general reflections of their time on the EBS.

Table 2.2 Interviewees by area

	Bradford	Hull	Leeds	Scarborough	Sheffield	York	SN	Total
Courts								
District judges	1	1	3	0	2	0	0	7
Magistrates	6	6	6	4	6	4	0	2
Legal advisors	2	3	3	2	2	2	0	4
CPS	2	4	4	1	2	2	0	5
Defence solicitors	1	2	2	1	2	2	0	0
Senior probation officers	1	1	1	1	1	1	0	6
Workers								
Accommo-dation officers	1	1	2	0	1	1	0	6
Bail information officers	1	1	2	1	1	0	0	6
Bail support officers	1	1	1	1	1	1	1	7
Mentors	4	4	4	3	3	3	0	1
Defendants	8	7	9	5	8	6	1	4

3

The Effective Bail Scheme in Yorkshire and Humberside

The Effective Bail Scheme (EBS) was a bail support scheme for adults which operated in the Yorkshire and Humberside region between 2006 and 2010. It was originally set up as a pilot in six courts (Bradford, Hull, Leeds, Scarborough, Sheffield and York). The scheme was phased in between November 2006 and February 2007. During 2007 the scheme was expanded to several small courts covering rural areas in the region including Bingley in West Yorkshire. In late 2007, the scheme was expanded again to cover three further courts in North Yorkshire (Harrogate, Skipton and Northallerton (HSN). The courts were selected specifically to test the suitability of operating bail support schemes in urban and rural areas. This chapter describes the governance and staffing structures of the EBS and discusses some of the issues which arose with these aspects of the scheme. Before this, the role of the Bail Information Pathfinder (BIP) is discussed.

The Bail Information Pathfinder

Alongside the EBS, the Yorkshire and Humberside Regional Offender Manager commissioned a pilot bail information scheme funded by the national Pathfinder initiative (Brown et al, 2008). The scheme began in November 2006 and ran alongside the EBS. Although, the BIP was a separate initiative with a different funding source, its role as gatekeeper to the EBS was crucial. It basically assessed defendants' suitability for the EBS making it impossible to separate the impact of one scheme from the other.

The BIP identified defendants at risk of custodial remands prior to their first court appearance and interviewed them to ascertain information relevant to the remand decision. Where appropriate, information, which was verified where possible, was provided to the court with copies usually also given to the Crown Prosecution Service and defence solicitors. In this respect, the BIP differed from previous bail information schemes in England and Wales where the primary recipients were the CPS and not the court (see Chapter One). The information provided by the BIP included information about defendants' community ties as well as details of any bail support package and/or available accommodation when appropriate.

The aim of the scheme was to improve the quality and quantity of information available to the court in order to increase the reliability of remand decisions. It also counterbalanced Crown Prosecution Service (CPS) objections to bail aiming to increase the number of defendants bailed rather than remanded in custody. An in-house evaluation of the scheme suggested that custodial remands reduced in courts where the scheme operated but only when the EBS scheme was also available, suggesting that both schemes were required to reduce custodial remands (Brown et al, 2008). Stakeholders appeared to support the necessity of having both bail information and bail support schemes but court and Crown Prosecution staff indicated that the bail information scheme had benefits independent of bail support schemes, suggesting that they save court time and provide valuable objective information. Such views echo previous research findings on the value of bail information schemes (for example, Hucklesby, 1994b; Lloyd, 1992). During the pilot, views differed about the role of bail information. All bail information officers used it to assess and offer bail support where appropriate but in some areas bail information was provided to the courts even when bail support was not offered to the court. It was in this broader role, as information provider, rather than simply a bail support referrer, that the CPS particularly welcomed the scheme.

According to Brown and colleagues (2008) the impact of the Yorkshire and Humberside scheme varied between courts with schemes with lower workloads having the greatest impact on custodial remand rates. This might be explained by a number of factors including awareness of the scheme among court actors, the frequency and quality of personal contact between bail information staff and court actors, differences in levels of court actors' trust and legitimacy of the scheme and the workload of the bail information staff.

After 18 months, funding for the BIP ceased. In April 2008, three probation areas/ trusts funded four full-time bail information posts (in Bradford, Hull, Leeds and Sheffield). In North Yorkshire the role was subsumed into court teams where two different models for operating the service ran. One involved bail information being provided by the generic court team with no individual taking responsibility for it. The second model involved the employment of a fractional bail information officer who was embedded in the court team and who also had additional duties. Although not statistically verified, interviewees suggested that the second model had better referral rates and ensured that the bail information role was done.

The next section introduces the EBS which provided bail support and accommodation in Yorkshire and Humberside.

The Effective Bail Scheme

The EBS was set up as a result of a successful bid to the Treasury Invest to Save Budget (ISB). It aimed to pilot arrangements for the provision of bail support for adult defendants (NOMS, 2007). The officially stated aims were to:

- help defendants on bail comply with conditions and attend court when required;
- support defendants on bail in the community by helping them to handle their contact with government agencies, enabling them to reduce the likelihood of breaching conditions and offending; and
- provide accommodation for defendants on bail which meets the needs of the courts (NOMS, 2007: 1).

The implicit aim of the scheme was to divert defendants away from custodial remands in order to reduce the prison remand population. This would be achieved by providing reassurances to the courts that defendants would be in touch with the scheme throughout the time that they were on bail. The regular contact between defendants and the scheme would reduce the risk of non-compliance and the likelihood of further offending. There was also an expectation that defendants would receive assistance with needs identified by the scheme. Some defendants would also be accommodated by the scheme thus reducing the risk of absconding and offending in some cases.

The target population for the EBS were cases in which defendants were detained by the police to appear at magistrates' courts and the Crown Prosecution Service (CPS) were intending to object to bail: in short, defendants who were at risk of a custodial remand. In practice, the first of these criteria was nearly always strictly adhered to and sometimes used as a proxy for the second. By contrast the second criterion was not always met because time did not always permit workers to check whether the CPS intended to object to bail. Defendants were identified from lists of overnight cases received from the police or by staff in court cells alerting bail information staff to potential candidates. Once identified bail information officers carried out preliminary inquiries such as whether they were already known to the Probation Service before interviewing defendants. Which defendants were interviewed varied between courts. In some courts, bail information officers aimed to interview all defendants who were in the cells. In others, workers made judgements about whom they should see. Interviews included a brief summary of the purpose of the scheme followed by questions about the defendants offending and bail record and their personal circumstances and community ties. In cases where defendants were deemed suitable and eligible for the EBS, reports were provided to the court, Crown Prosecution Service and defence solicitors recommending bail support and detailing defendants' circumstances. Where deemed necessary by bail information officers, accommodation was also offered as part of the bail support package. The courts would then decide whether to impose bail support as a condition of bail. Once imposed defendants were required to attend three appointments per week and reside at the accommodation provided by the scheme if the courts deemed this necessary. Consequently, the EBS provided either support only packages or an accommodation and support package. Support was primarily provided by paid staff with the assistance of volunteer mentors. Process maps can be found in Appendix One.

Management of the Effective Bail Scheme

The EBS was a multi-agency partnership between the National Offender Management Service (NOMS) and the voluntary sector. The EBS provided an opportunity to test out how these policy objectives might work in practice at a time when contestability and increasing voluntary sector involvement in the provision of criminal justice services were firmly on the Labour government's agenda. To this end, one of the stated aims of the scheme was to 'test and develop the collaboration and governance of multi-tiered voluntary sector partnerships with some agencies as partners and suppliers' (NOMS, 2007: 1). The scheme was run by three voluntary sector organisations. Nacro was the lead agency providing day-to-day support to defendants; Foundation Housing managed the accommodation provision; and SOVA managed the mentoring aspect of the scheme.

The EBS had a three-tier governance structure. Overseeing the operation of the EBS was the Partnership Board which was chaired by the Regional Offender Manager and attended by senior representatives of statutory sector agencies, the Ministry of Justice and the partner agencies running the scheme. The Operational Management Group was chaired by Nacro and its membership included representatives from partner agencies, the Regional Offender Manager's Office, the sponsor at NOMS Headquarters, probation areas and the evaluation team. The purpose of this group was to oversee the operation of the scheme and identify and deal with any problems which arose. Local Advisory Groups operated in each court area, were chaired by Nacro and their membership included local workers, mentoring coordinators, the accommodation managers and representatives from local statutory agencies. The purpose of these groups was to inform local statutory agencies about the how the scheme was progressing and iron out any problems which arose. The governance structure for the EBS was viewed positively by interviewees although there were some concerns that the Partnership Board failed to fully fulfil its accountability function.

Staffing

Figure 3.1 is an organisational chart of the EBS. It shows that each court had a core team of three workers: a bail support officer who managed the support element of the scheme, an accommodation officer who managed the accommodation and also supported defendants who were housed by the scheme, and a bail information officer who assessed defendants while in custody and provided reports to the courts. Later on in the pilot, a single worker was employed to work in the courts of Harrogate, Skipton and Northallerton where she undertook all of the roles of the court teams in other areas. Above the court teams were three individuals – two senior practitioners and an accommodation manager. The senior practitioners oversaw the bail information officers and the bail support officers while the accommodation manager managed the accommodation and the accommodation workers in each of the court teams. All three of these senior posts were intended to have developmental and strategic roles but the senior practitioners in particular spent most of their time supervising staff and dealing with staffing issues. Two mentoring coordinators were also employed to manage the mentoring element of the scheme. A project manager had overall responsibility for running the EBS. What complicated this hierarchical arrangement was that staff were employed by different agencies which led to divergences in salaries, terms and conditions and management. The accommodation manager and officers were employed directly by Foundation Housing. Bail support officers, the senior practitioners and the project manager were employed by Nacro. The bail information officers were seconded to Nacro from the probation areas/trusts. However they were routinely managed by the Senior Probation Officers in the court teams leading to one Probation Assistant Chief Officer commenting that it was 'a secondment in name rather than anything else'. While staff on the ground were happy with how these arrangements operated, they had resource implications for probation teams and this sometimes caused friction between Nacro and probation staff. Finally, the two mentoring coordinators were employees of SOVA and were managed by a regional manager. The complicated management arrangements resulted in some problems which militated against joint working and a sense of shared ownership and responsibility. A second complicating factor in the staffing arrangements was the regional nature of the EBS resulting in a large geographic area being covered. This meant that court teams rarely had contact with each other and their managers spent considerable time travelling between courts so that they were rarely together in the project office. This made communications between staff difficult and in some cases sporadic.

Figure 3.1 Organisational chart of the Effective Bail Scheme (June 2008)

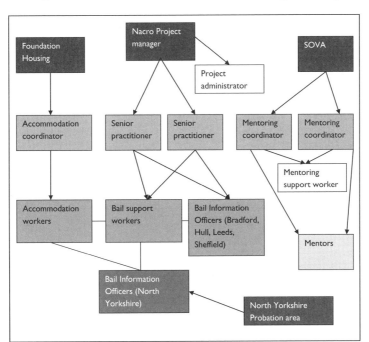

The staffing structure of the EBS was inflexible. The deployment of the same number of staff and the same staffing structure in the each of the six main courts raised considerable issues during the pilot. The original staffing structure took no account of different caseloads within the courts. Consequently, while staff in some courts struggled to meet demand, others were not fully employed. Later on in the pilot, changes were made to accommodate differences in workloads by employing additional project staff in the busier courts but the inflexibility of the structure continued to present problems. The three types of staff (bail information officer, bail support officer and accommodation officer) also remained discrete throughout the duration of the project which contributed to problems dealing with the peaks and dips in workloads. Staff generally did not take on each others' roles even when one worker was struggling to manage their caseload while another member of the team had capacity or when workers were absent.

Facilities

The facilities available to project staff varied between areas as did their location. This was largely dictated by the space available at courts and in probation offices. At the start of the project, it had been suggested that the probation areas would accommodate staff within their court teams. Generally, all or some of the project staff were located within probation facilities either at courts or in offices nearby. Nonetheless, some probation managers raised concerns about their resources being used for the scheme without recognition or reimbursement.

In two areas all of the project team were located together. This resulted in a much greater level of integration, team working and efficiency and had considerable pay-offs in terms of staff morale, workload management, communication and so on. The location of workers was key to the efficient and effective operation of the scheme and it was clear that the ideal scenario is for the whole team to be located in magistrates' courts although this only happened in one area.

This chapter has examined the genesis and organisational structure of both the BIP and the EBS. In the next chapter, data on the operation of the EBS will be discussed.

The operation of the Effective Bail Scheme

This chapter examines data relating to the operation of the EBS and its component parts between its implementation and the end of June 2008. It explores take-up of the scheme and the caseload of the EBS in different court areas throughout this period. The second part of the chapter examines the demographic characteristics of defendants as well as their current offences and offending and bail histories. It also explores differences in these factors between defendants who were bailed to the EBS and those who were remanded in custody in order to begin to understand why some proposals for bail support failed. Data presented in this chapter were gleaned from bail information and bail support records.

Figure 4.1 provides details of the process which resulted in 658 defendants being bailed with EBS. Bail information officers initially identified 1,417 defendants who may have been eligible for the EBS because they were detained in police custody while awaiting their first court appearance or because they had been remanded in custody at an earlier hearing.

In over a third (n=523, 37%) of cases no proposal for bail support was submitted to the courts. Three-quarters (n=398, 76%) of this group were deemed to be either unsuitable, ineligible or both for the EBS. There is some overlap between the two categories. In terms of unsuitability, the most frequently cited reasons were that defendants had no support needs (n=22), there were concerns about manageability (n=15) or no suitable accommodation was available (n=12).[1] In terms of ineligibility, the most frequently cited reason was that defendants were ineligible for Restriction on Bail (RoB) (n=99).[2] A policy decision was made early on in the pilot that defendants who tested positive for a specified Class A drug at the police station and who were therefore eligible for RoB could not be offered bail support. This decision was taken because of concerns about duplication of work and overburdening defendants. Consequently, most RoB-eligible cases were screened out before bail information officers interviewed defendants. However, nearly without exception, interviewees advocated that decision-makers should be able to impose RoB and bail support conditions together. The reasons given for this were that there was no accommodation provided by the Drug Interventions Programme (DIP) and that there was uncertainty about the level of support offered by DIP other than in relation to drug treatment. Interviewees also believed that imposing both conditions simultaneously would reduce custodial remands, and data support this view. Just over a quarter (n=48, 28%) of defendants remanded in custody after being deemed ineligible and/or unsuitable for EBS were originally identified as eligible for RoB.[3] This suggests that enabling EBS and RoB to be applied simultaneously may reduce the number of custodial remands.

Figure 4.1 Number of defendants receiving EBS at different stages of the remand process

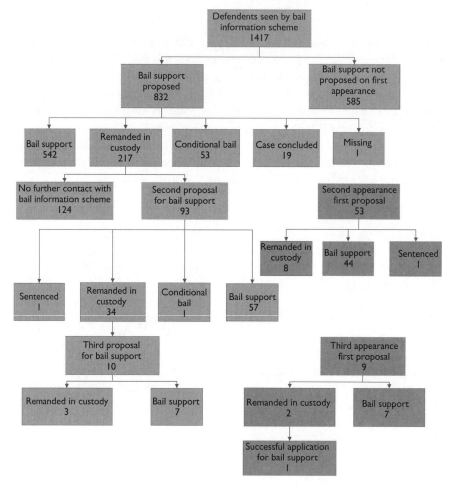

Figure 4.2 provides details of the remand outcomes for defendants in cases in which no proposal for EBS was made to the courts. It demonstrates that over two-fifths (n=174, 44%) of the defendants who were deemed unsuitable and/or ineligible for EBS were remanded in custody. In just under a fifth (n=90, 17%) of cases where no proposals for EBS were made, defendants were deemed eligible and suitable for bail support.[4] In nearly two-fifths (n=33, 37%) of these cases defendants were remanded in custody but a significant minority (n=42, 47%) were remanded on bail, mostly with conditions (n=41).[5]

In nearly two-thirds (n=894, 63%) of cases, a bail support package was proposed to the courts by bail information officers for the first time at the defendant's first (n=832), second (n=53) or third appearance (n=9) (see Figure 4.1). Two-thirds (n=593, 66%) of these proposals resulted in bail support being imposed. In terms of the other cases, a quarter (n=227, 25%) of defendants were remanded in custody and a small number (n=53) were remanded on conditional bail without bail support. Together these figures suggest that proposals for bail support were reasonably well targeted towards those at risk of a custodial remand. In nearly half (n=104, 46%) of cases in which defendants were remanded in custody at their first appearance after EBS had been proposed, further proposals for EBS were put forward at subsequent court hearings. This resulted in an additional 64 (7%) defendants being granted bail with bail support conditions.

Figure 4.2 Remand decisions for defendants in cases where no proposal for EBS was made to the courts

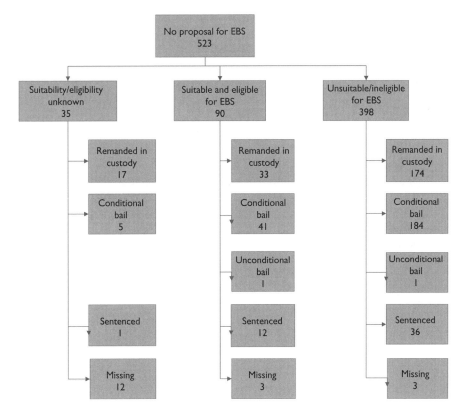

Bail conditions

Most defendants who had bail support imposed also had other bail conditions attached. Only 29 defendants were known not to have bail conditions imposed.[6] The majority of defendants had two (n=220, 34%) or three (n=193, 30%) additional bail conditions imposed. Over a tenth (n=78, 12%) of defendants had more than four additional bail conditions. These findings are similar to previous research (see, for example, Hucklesby, 1994a; Raine and Willson, 1994, 1996). Table 4.1 shows that the majority of defendants (n=585, 89%) had to abide by residence conditions including 237 defendants who were accommodated by the EBS.[7] In nearly half (n=310, 47%) of the cases, defendants were required to have no contact with particular people which is likely to reflect the prevalence of domestic violence cases in the sample (see below). The use of specific conditions mirrors the findings of previous research (see Hucklesby, 1994a; Morgan and Henderson, 1998; Airs et al, 2000). The low number of defendants (n=7) who also had an RoB condition imposed is explained by the EBS policy of not offering RoB and EBS simultaneously to courts (see Hucklesby et al, 2008).

Table 4.1 shows that curfews with and without electronic monitoring (EM) were used in around a third of cases (n=209, 32%) which is broadly in line with some previous research findings (see, for example, Hucklesby, 1994a). Curfew hours were recorded in 133 cases. In nearly all cases, curfews were overnight. In over half of the cases (n=76, 57%) curfews were for a period of 12 hours.[8] In just under a fifth (n=113, 17%) of cases defendants were subject to electronically monitored curfew conditions at the hearing in which bail support was also imposed. However, 125 defendants were subject to electronically monitored curfew conditions sometime during the period they were on the EBS.

Table 4.1 Bail conditions used initially in bail support cases

	Number	Percentage N=6471
Residence	548	85
Bail support accommodation	237	37
Other residence	311	48
No contact	310	48
Exclusion from place	265	41
Curfew with EM	113	17
Curfew	96	15
Reporting	84	13
Comply with preparation of report	27	4
Restriction on bail	7	1
Address substance misuse/cooperate with testing	6	1
Other	27	4
Total	**1,483**	

Note: Information about bail conditions is missing in 11 cases.

Substantial differences existed in the use of EM curfew conditions between areas. In Scarborough, two-fifths (n=28, 40%) of EBS cases also had EM curfew conditions imposed compared with less than a tenth (n=9, 8%) in Hull. Interviews in Scarborough suggested that bail information officers were routinely recommending to courts that EM curfews were imposed in EBS cases and that magistrates believed that they were a mandatory part of the scheme (see Hucklesby et al, 2008). These data appear to confirm the consequences of this practice. Another measure of the use of EM curfews is to compare the number of curfews with and without EM in each area. This shows a different pattern although large variations still existed between areas.[9]

It was impossible to assess the interactive effects of imposing EM curfews alongside bail support conditions. Very little information about EM conditions was recorded in EBS files and it is not certain that the records kept by the EBS are accurate. G4S kept records of defendants on the EBS who were also subject to EM curfews but data were only available in 85 cases.

EBS caseloads

The courts bailed 658 defendants to the EBS from the start of the scheme to 30 June 2008 but supervised 655 cases.[10] This included 625 individual defendants, because 30 defendants were on the scheme more than once for different sets of offences.[11] Take-up during this period was lower than the target figure of 600 commencements per year[12] and varied between areas. Table 4.2 provides a breakdown of cases by area. It demonstrates that Leeds and Sheffield accounted for nearly half of the cases (n=306, 47%) supervised by the scheme while North Yorkshire (Harrogate, Skipton, Northallerton, Scarborough and York) accounted for a fifth of cases (n=128, 20%). Some, but not all of the caseload differential reflects variations in the number of cases appearing in the courts which in turn is linked to the nature of the court environs (that is, whether they were urban or rural courts). The busier courts also had District Judges regularly dealing with remand courts whose knowledge of, and confidence in, the EBS was greater than magistrates, making it more likely that they would use the scheme (Hucklesby et al, 2008).

Table 4.2 Number of cases by area

	Number	Percentage
Bradford	103	16
Hull	118	18
Leeds	157	24
Scarborough	70	11
Sheffield	149	23
York	47	7
Harrogate, Skipton and Northallerton (HSN)	11	2
Total	**655**	**100**

Figure 4.3 shows the number of commencements on the scheme (statistics for different courts can be found in Appendix Two). The mean number of commencements was 43 per month throughout the whole pilot period. It might be expected as the scheme became better known that the number of commencements would increase over time. However, the mean number of commencements in the six months prior to June 2008 was 38, lower than the overall figure. Figure 4.3 demonstrates that there were wide fluctuations in the number of new commencements over the period of the pilot.[13] The mean number of commencements in the different courts varied widely also from 1.57 in HSN (Harrogate, Skipton and Northallerton) to 7.85 in Leeds partly reflecting the amount of business in different courts.[14] The target for the scheme was two commencements in each court per week. This target was missed and was reached in only three out of the 20 months of operation covered by this report. There were wide fluctuations in the number of new starts per month within the areas.[15] Only Leeds, the largest and busiest court, consistently reached its target for commencements in the six months to June 2008 (see Appendix Two).

Figure 4.3 Total number of commencements on the EBS

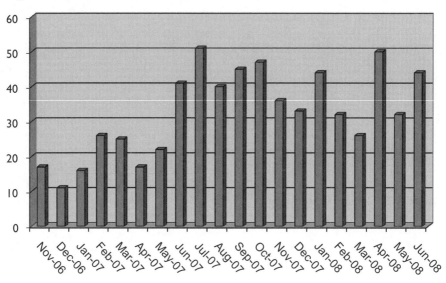

Figure 4.4 shows overall caseloads for the EBS throughout the period. It demonstrates that caseloads increased steadily until October 2007 after which they levelled off at between 118 and 140 cases at any one time. The mean caseload for the six months to June 2008 was 127 cases. However, there were wide variations in caseloads between areas with the two busy urban courts (Leeds and Sheffield) having significantly higher caseloads than Bradford and Hull and the North Yorkshire courts (see Appendix Three).[16] This demonstrates that staffing structures need to take account of different caseloads rather than working within a rather crude 'one size fits all' model as the project did throughout this period.[17] Caseloads fluctuated also within areas over time but not to any significant extent in the six months to June 2008.

Caseloads are affected by the number of defendants joining the scheme and also the length of time spent on it. The mean number of days spent on the scheme was 64. This is significantly longer than the 49 days envisaged in the original ISB bid and explains why caseload was higher than expected despite commencements not reaching their target level. It is unclear how the original estimates were derived although they reflect the annual average time spent on remand at the time the bid was submitted, but it is of some concern that defendants spent longer on the scheme than originally envisaged. The length of time spent on the scheme largely reflects how long cases take to complete but it is possible that courts were less vigilant about dealing with cases expeditiously because defendants were on bail and/or receiving assistance and support. The number of days spent on the EBS ranged from zero to 380 (just over one year). Differences existed between areas both in terms of ranges and means.[18] The higher caseloads in Leeds and Sheffield (see Appendix Three) appear to be a function of both the higher number of defendants joining the scheme and the longer time spent on the scheme in these areas.

Figure 4.4: EBS caseload

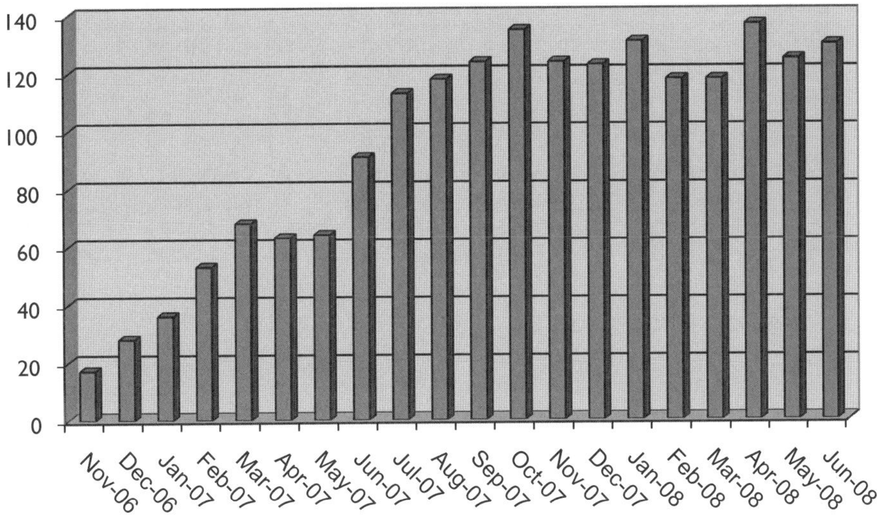

EBS accommodation

The accommodation status of defendants was assessed by bail information staff prior to making offers of bail support to courts. At this time over two-thirds (n=456, 69%) of defendants who were subsequently given bail support were identified as having an address. A total of 120 defendants were identified as being of no fixed abode with a slightly higher number (n=144, 22%) assessed as having no suitable bail address. However, the courts required over twice as many defendants to be accommodated by the scheme. This suggests either that the assessment process was not robust enough or that courts required defendants to be accommodated by the EBS when they had an alternative address.

In just over two-fifths (n=275, 42%) of cases defendants were accommodated by the scheme. Figure 4.5 demonstrates that the number of defendants accommodated remained relatively stable at between 45 and 55 between September 2007 and June 2008, but varied between (see Appendix Four)[19] and within areas over the time (see Appendix Five). There is some evidence that EBS accommodation was used to ensure that some defendants were accommodated away from where the alleged offences took place which was heralded by remand decision-makers as one of the advantages of the EBS especially in cases of domestic violence (see Hucklesby et al, 2008).[20]

Figure 4.5 Number of defendants accommodated by the EBS

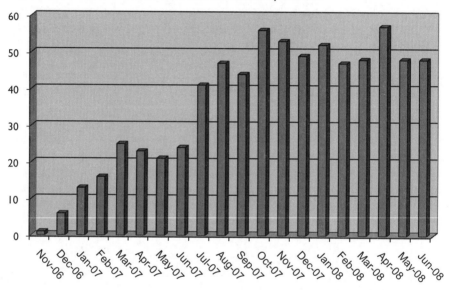

An important question raised by these data is whether all the defendants who were accommodated by the EBS required it. It is impossible to assess this accurately but data provides some indication that not all defendants may have required EBS accommodation. There are a number of sources of data which overlap. Bail information staff assessed nearly half (n=122, 47%) of the defendants who were accommodated as having suitable accommodation. There were differences between areas.[21] Nearly half (n=119, 46%) of defendants had an address at the time they were assessed by bail information officers. It is acknowledged that some of this accommodation would be viewed as unsuitable by the court for a variety of reasons. However, over half (n=64, 54%) of the defendants who were assessed as having suitable accommodation lived in their own homes or stable rented accommodation. A further seven defendants were already living in specialist accommodation for offenders. This suggests that courts may have been utilising EBS accommodation when it was unnecessary resulting in net-widening. In this context net-widening takes place when defendants are put on the scheme who would have been remanded on bail without EBS if the EBS did not exist, thereby increasing the requirements that they have to abide by and the intensity of their contact with the criminal justice system. Net-widening wastes resources, raises human rights issues and potentially up-tariffs defendants making it more likely that they would be remanded in custody as a result of breaches or further alleged offending, therefore, potentially increasing the prison population.

The use of accommodation fluctuated within areas over time resulting in a lack of capacity at some times and costly voids and under-occupancy at others (see Appendix Five). During the pilot, each area had its own accommodation which was largely managed locally. A more centralised system of accommodation provision is likely to enhance flexibility and may reduce resource use. The disadvantage of such an approach would be that defendants may have to be accommodated away from their 'home' area making continuity of service provision more challenging. Conversely, accommodating defendants away from their 'home' area can be advantageous where the courts require defendants to be housed away from the area in which they allegedly offended.[22] This was one of the advantages of a regional scheme and worked well in the small number of cases where it was required although logistical difficulties were reported including defendants arriving at accommodation out of normal working hours.

Accommodation data were compiled by Foundation Housing and were available in the majority of cases (n=265).[23] They show that defendants' stays in accommodation ranged from one day to 327 days (around 11 months) with the mean length of stay being 61 days. Lengths of stays in EBS accommodation varied between areas.[24] A third (n=87, 32%) of defendants left EBS accommodation before the end of their time on the EBS. A third (n=88, 32%) of defendants remained in EBS accommodation after the end of their bail period and some for a substantial period of time.[25] EBS accommodation was provided as short-hold tenancies for a period of six months so it was always envisaged that some defendants would remain in EBS accommodation after their bail period had ended. However, data suggest that more permanent accommodation was unavailable in some cases when it was required. This had implications for the availability of accommodation for other defendants and may have contributed to the logistical challenges of managing accommodation provision.

Around a fifth (n=58, 22%) of defendants accommodated by the scheme were housed in self-contained single accommodation. A further two-fifths (n=112, 42%) were housed in shared accommodation. The use of shared accommodation raises a number of issues including increasing difficulties with managing capacity and voids because some defendants could not be housed together as well as managing the behaviour of defendants. The remaining (n=95, 36%) defendants were accommodated in bed and breakfast accommodation. The high use of bed and breakfast accommodation raises questions about the suitability of this type of accommodation for defendants on bail especially when decision-makers often believed that specialist accommodation was being used (see Hucklesby et al, 2008). The use of different types of accommodation varied between areas. In Scarborough nearly all (n=44, 96%) accommodation was bed and breakfast. This compares with York, Hull and Sheffield where this type of accommodation was used minimally. Bed and breakfast accommodation was only used in two cases across these three sites. The highest proportion of single accommodation was used in Hull (n=31, 82%). Usually between 10% and 20% of defendants were housed in single accommodation in most areas. The use of shared accommodation was highest in Sheffield and York (88% and 85% respectively).

Defendants' characteristics

Having described the use of the EBS in the first part of this chapter, this section examines the characteristics of the defendants on the scheme and, where applicable, those who were remanded but not to the EBS.

Age

The mean age of defendants on the scheme was 27 with ages ranging from 17 to 74. The mean age of defendants did not vary much between areas.[26] The mean age of those offered but not granted bail support was slightly lower, at 26, but the mean age of defendants for whom bail support was not offered to courts was 30. This suggests that bail information officers are more likely to offer bail support to younger defendants, reflecting policy guidance, although they may also have less serious or persistent offending and/or bail histories.

Gender

Most cases involved male defendants (n=597, 91%). The number of cases involving women was small (n=61) so findings need to be treated cautiously. There were differences in the proportion of women on the EBS between areas.[27] Table 4.3 shows the representation of women at different stages of the EBS process. It suggests that the proportion of women on the EBS was in line with the number of women who were detained by the police. It also suggests that when bail support was proposed to courts in cases involving women it was usually successful, suggesting that there may be more scope for EBS to be proposed for female defendants.

Table 4.3 Gender breakdown of defendants at different stages of the EBS process

	Men		Women	
	N	%	N	%
EBS not proposed	471	90	52	10
Proposal for EBS rejected	224	95	12	5
EBS imposed	597	91	61	9
Total	**1,292**	**91**	**125**	**9**

Half of the cases in which the EBS was not proposed for both men (n=212, 50%) and women (n=54, 50%) resulted in custodial remands and a similar number were bailed conditionally. A higher proportion of women (n=21, 47%) than men (n=78, 22%) were assessed as ineligible for EBS because they were eligible for RoB. Nine of these women were subsequently remanded in custody which suggests that there is potential to increase the number of women diverted from custodial remands by EBS and RoB being made available together. For women, half (n=6) of EBS proposals were rejected and resulted in custodial remands.[28] The rest were conditionally bailed suggesting that there were some issues about targeting EBS proposals and the potential for net-widening to occur. Such concerns were heightened in cases involving women.

Ethnicity

Table 4.4 shows the ethnicity of defendants on the EBS. It demonstrates that just over a tenth (n=75, 11%) of defendants were from BME groups. The representation of BME defendants was lower than might be expected given their representation in the prison remand population (between 16 and 18% depending on the ethnic group) leading to some concern that they may be under-represented on the EBS (Ministry of Justice, 2009b). Table 4.4 demonstrates that the proportion of BME defendants who were subject to bail support was lower than the proportion of defendants from these groups who were detained in police custody or whose EBS proposals were rejected. It appears, therefore, that part of the explanation for the lower than expected representation of BME groups on the EBS was that courts were not accepting proposals for bail support. A number of factors may contribute to this finding including that defendants from BME backgrounds were charged with more serious offences, had more serious offending or bail histories or the police or CPS were more likely to apply for custodial remands.[29] Yet it is also possible that bail information reports were not as detailed and/or persuasive in cases involving BME defendants which is an issue highlighted in relation to court reports prepared by the Probation Service (HMIPro, 2000; Hudson and Bramhall, 2005). An option for increasing the representation of BME defendants on the EBS is to increase the number of proposals for EBS presented to courts. One way of doing this, while limiting the potential for net-widening, would be to broaden the criteria for selection by increasing the threshold of seriousness for cases involving BME defendants.[30]

Table 4.4 Ethnicity breakdown of defendants at different stages of the EBS process[31, 32]

	White		BME	
	N	%	N	%
EBS not proposed	446	87	68[1]	13
Proposal for EBS rejected	198	84	38[2]	16
EBS imposed	584	89	75	11
Total	**1,228**	**87**	**181**	**13**

Table 4.5 shows that there were differences between areas in terms of the proportion of defendants from BME groups supervised by the scheme. The highest proportion of BME defendants on EBS was in Sheffield (n=29, 19%). The low number of BME defendants in Hull, Scarborough and HSN is probably explained by the predominantly White populations in these areas. Numbers are small but there were also some differences between areas in the ethnic groups who were represented on the EBS. Table 4.5 shows that Sheffield was the most ethnically diverse defendant population while Asians predominated in Bradford as would be expected from the make up of the Cities' populations.

Table 4.5 Ethnicity of defendants on the EBS

	White		Black		Asian		Mixed		Other		BME Total	
	N	%	N	%	N	%	N	%	N	%	N	%
Bradford	88	85	2	2	11	11	2	2	0	0	15	15
Hull	116	98	1	1	0	0	1	1	0	0	2	2
Leeds	135	87	10	6	5	3	6	4	0	0	21	13
Scarborough	69	99	0	0	0	0	1	1	0	0	2	3
Sheffield	120	81	13	9	6	4	8	5	2	1	29	19
York	45	96	0	0	0	0	2	4	0	0	6	13
HSN	11	100	0	0	0	0	0	0	0	0	0	0
Total	**584**	**89**	**26**	**4**	**22**	**3**	**20**	**3**	**2**	**<1**	**75**	**11**

Alleged offences

Defendants in the sample were charged with a wide range of offences. Table 4.6 provides details of the most serious offence with which defendants were charged.[33] The largest number of defendants were charged with offences of battery (n=111, 17%) followed by burglary (n=88, 13%) and serious violence including wounding and GBH (n=80, 12%). This suggests that the scheme was used for defendants charged with serious offences such as those presented above in around two-fifths of cases and gives an indication that it was used for some defendants who were likely to have been at risk of custodial remands. Conversely, a small group of defendants on the EBS were charged with low tariff offences including shoplifting, section four and five public order offences and for being drunk and disorderly which would not normally be expected to result in custodial remands, suggesting that some net-widening occurred.

Domestic violence was a feature of many alleged offences and this was not only for the charge of battery. Some property offences were clearly linked to incidents of a domestic nature and some breaches of orders were related to injunctions to keep away from partners or ex-partners. The police identified a fifth (n=142, 22%) of offences as 'domestic'. The prevalence of offences involving domestic violence in EBS cases may be linked to the availability of accommodation because many of these defendants would have been unable to return to their usual residence leaving them without a bail address.

Table 4.6 Main alleged offence

	EBS imposed		EBS proposed outcome RIC		RIC no EBS proposal	
	N	%	N	%	N	%
Offences against the person						
Battery	111	17	19	13	25	11
Serious violence	80	12	37	25	45	20
ABH	51	8	8	5	10	4
Less serious violence	22	3	0	0	3	1
Sex offences	9	1	0	0	13	6
Total offences against the person	273	42	64	44	96	43
Property offences						
Burglary	88	13	26	18	23	10
Theft, deception and fraud	52	8	5	3	16	7
Shoplifting	51	8	9	6	14	6
Other property	20	3	3	2	3	1
Arson	4	1	0	0	3	1
Total property offences	215	33	43	29	59	26
Breach of bail	33	5	5	3	3	1
Drugs	24	4	5	3	22	10
Vehicle crime	20	3	7	5	13	6
Driving	20	3	1	1	2	1
Offensive weapon	22	3	5	3	8	4
Breach of other order	19	3	9	6	5	2
Other	29	4	8	5	16	7
Total	**655**	**100**	**147**	**100**	**224**	**100**

Table 4.6 also compares main offences for defendants granted bail with EBS and defendants remanded in custody with and without proposals for EBS. Findings need to be treated cautiously because of the small number of some offences. However a number of important differences existed between the groups. First, the proportion of defendants charged with battery who were bailed with EBS was higher than either of the groups who were remanded in custody. Conversely, the proportion of defendants charged with serious violence was higher for both groups who were remanded in custody. This suggests that both bail information staff and courts considered the nature and seriousness of offences against the person when making decisions about whether to propose or impose bail support conditions. Second, a higher proportion of defendants charged with property offences generally, and burglary in particular, had EBS proposed and subsequently imposed. Third, a higher proportion of defendants charged with drugs offences were remanded in custody. These findings demonstrate the influence of the nature and seriousness of offences on decisions to both propose and impose bail support conditions which confirms previous research findings (see, for example, Hucklesby, 1996; Morgan and Henderson, 1998). It also indicates that the more serious the alleged offences the less likely defendants were to be bailed onto the EBS.

Table 4.7 demonstrates that the mix of alleged offences for which defendants on the EBS were charged varied between areas.[34] Table 4.7 shows that the proportion of defendants on the EBS charged with battery varied from a quarter (n=37, 25%) in Sheffield to a tenth (n=12, 11%) in Bradford and the proportion of defendants charged with serious violence varied from a tenth in Hull (n=11, 9%) to two-fifths (n=31, 20%) in Leeds. Notable is the high number of defendants (n=15, 21%) who had EBS imposed for breach of bail in Scarborough despite the existence of policy that EBS should not be proposed for this group. It is difficult to draw firm conclusions because numbers are relatively small, but based on the nature and seriousness of alleged offences, Table 4.7 suggests that there were area variations in the proportion of defendants on the EBS who may have been at risk of custodial remands.

Table 4.7 Main alleged offence by area[35]

	Bradford		Hull		Leeds		Scarborough		Sheffield		York	
	N	%	N	%	N	%	N	%	N	%	N	%
Battery	12	11	20	17	22	14	10	14	37	25	8	17
Serious violence	11	11	11	9	31	20	7	10	15	10	5	11
Actual bodily harm	9	9	11	9	13	8	2	3	14	9	1	2
Burglary	25	24	8	7	34	22	1	1	11	7	7	15
Breach of bail	2	2	4	3	0	0	15	21	6	4	6	13

Criminal justice related information

Criminal justice related information about the EBS was available from the data recorded during the bail information assessment and from official sources such as previous convictions records and police paperwork.[36] Table 4.8 provides details of the extent to which defendants had criminal justice histories which would potentially put them at greater risk of custodial remands (based on previous research see, for example, Hucklesby, 1996, 1997a; Morgan and Henderson, 1998). It also provides comparisons between cases in which defendants had EBS imposed and defendants who were remanded in custody with or without proposals for EBS being made. It demonstrates a number of points. First, defendants who had EBS imposed had less serious offending and bail histories than defendants whose EBS proposal was rejected.[37] Second, there were differences in the police and Crown Prosecution Service (CPS) requests between those on the EBS and those who had EBS proposed but who were remanded in custody. The police requested custodial remands in nearly all cases for both groups but they also provided details of bail conditions which they deemed appropriate in a much higher number of cases in which EBS was subsequently imposed (98%) than when defendants were subsequently remanded in custody (65%). The CPS were more likely to have requested custodial remands in cases where proposals for EBS were rejected rather than accepted (85% compared with 97%). This indicates that proposals for EBS were more likely to succeed when defendants had less serious offending and bail histories and when the police and CPS were less averse to defendants being bailed. This highlights the need to engage with both the police and CPS to promote the EBS and other community-based alternatives in order to reduce their applications for custodial remands.

Table 4.8 The prevalence of factors linked with custodial remands among defendants on the EBS and those remanded in custody with and without an EBS proposal

	EBS imposed		EBS proposed outcome RIC		RIC no EBS proposal	
	N	%	N	%	N	%
Previous convictions	N= 588		N=90		N=157	
None	43	7	7	4	13	8
Yes	545	93	83	92	144	92
1–5	148	27	17	20	7	5
6–10	118	22	15	18	10	7
11–20	139	26	25	30	18	13
21+	140	26	26	31	65	45
Unknown	0		0		44	31
Previous custodial sentence	N=550		N=83		N=150	
No	212	39	21	25	37	25
Yes	338	61	62	75	113	75
1	75	22	13	21	18	16
2–4	128	38	21	34	39	35
5+	130	38	25	40	56	50
Offending on bail	N=858		N=157		N=217	
Currently on bail	286	43	89	57	96	45
Previous offending on bail	241	37	97	61	100	65
On bail at time of offence	252	38	84	54	90	44
Record of failing to appear	N=858		N=157		N=217	
Failure to appear	87	13	28	18	33	16
Previous failure to appear	272	41	98	62	114	60
Record of breach of bail conditions	N=858		N=157		N=217	
Breach of bail	153	23	43	27	46	23
Previous breach of bail	103	16	31	20	32	32
Police bail decision	N=549		N=87		N=161	
Detained	522	95	82	94	153	95
Police remand recommendation	N=461		N=68		N=136	
Remand in custody	457	99	68	100	136	100
Alternative of bail conditions proposed	311	98	44	65	102	75
CPS remand request	N=618		N= 156		N=209	
Remand in custody	526	85	153	97	208	100
Conditional bail	6	1	0	0	1	>1
Bail support	86	14	3	3	0	0

The profile of defendants who were remanded in custody and had no proposal for EBS made to the court was similar in many ways to those who had proposals for EBS rejected by the courts. However, Table 4.8 demonstrates that are some important differences between the two groups of defendants which suggest that there may have been some potential for proposing EBS for this group. They were less likely to be on bail or to have committed their current offence on bail than those defendants who had EBS proposals rejected; and the police were more likely to hedge their bets by proposing conditions alongside a request for a custodial remand. Whether proposals for EBS are made is a difficult decision which involves trying to second guess courts' decisions. Yet these data suggest that broadening the criteria for making proposals may increase the numbers of defendants diverted from custodial remands. The risk is that it may result in net-widening.

This chapter has examined data on the operation of the EBS and provided a profile of the defendants who were granted bail to the EBS. In the next chapter, the work carried out by the EBS will be explored.

Notes

[1]   Other reasons included that no custodial remand application was being made (n=10), that defendants weren't interested (n=9); that defendants were too high risk (n=9), that only an address was required (n=6); mental health issues existed (n=7) or employment related issues (n=7).

[2]   Other reasons included: that they resided outside the EBS area (n=22); that no remand application was to be made (n=19); or that they had no support needs (n=12).

[3]   Only 28 of the 99 defendants identified as eligible for RoB were bailed with this condition.

[4]   Twelve of this group were recorded as being unwilling to comply with bail support.

[5]   A further 12 defendants were sentenced.

[6]   Analysis of the use of bail conditions is complicated by the fact that sometimes residence in bail support accommodation was made an explicit condition of bail (n=237) and in other cases it was not (n=38). For the purposes of this analysis the conditions of bail imposed by the court have been used. The number of defendants who did not have additional conditions attached to their bail increases to 77 if conditions of residence in bail support accommodation are excluded.

[7]   Courts did not always impose a residence condition on defendants accommodated by the scheme.

[8]   The lowest number of hours per curfew period was six but most curfews were between eight and 12 hours in length.

[9]   Two areas used EM curfews in the majority of cases where curfews were imposed (York, n=10, 66% and Bradford, n=17, 55%). In other areas, EM curfew were used in less than a fifth of cases in which curfews were imposed (Hull, n=9, 7%; Leeds, n=22, 18%).

[10] Three defendants were removed immediately from the scheme and no files existed for them. One defendant found an address outside of the EBS area; one defendant was profoundly deaf and could not be managed by the EBS; and one defendant was breached on the day that EBS was imposed.

[11] Twenty-eight defendants had been on the scheme twice, one defendant had been on the scheme three times and another one had been on it four times.

[12] As outlined in the bid to the Invest to Save Budget.

[13] In the year to June 2008, new starts per month ranged from 26 to 51 cases.

[14] The mean number of commencements in other courts was: Bradford 5.15; Hull 6.94; Scarborough 4.18; Sheffield 7.45; and York 2.76.

[15] For instance, the number of commencements varied from three to 14 in Sheffield and from three to 12 in Hull.

[16] The mean number of cases managed in Leeds in the six months to June 2008 was 36 compared with 21 in Hull and 7 in York.

[17] Each court had a bail support worker and an accommodation officer except for HSN where one bail support worker covered the whole area. For most of the pilot period, the six main courts also had dedicated bail information officers (see also Hucklesby et al, 2008).

[18] The mean number of days spent on the scheme excluding days spent in EBS accommodation after completion of the bail period in West Yorkshire (Bradford and Leeds) was 73 days compared with Scarborough where the mean was 39 days. This is compared with 68 days in Sheffield and 62 days in Hull. HSN and York were similar with defendants staying on the scheme for a mean time of 52 and 48 days respectively. The maximum number of days spent on the scheme excluding days spent in scheme accommodation after completion of the bail period also varied between areas from 380 days in Hull to 179 days in Scarborough and 128 days in HSN.

[19] The greatest use of accommodation was in Scarborough where defendants were accommodated in three quarters (n=53, 76%) of cases. This can be compared with Sheffield where defendants resided in EBS accommodation in just over a quarter (n=53, 28%) of cases.

[20] Eighteen defendants were accommodated outside of the original court area. In addition, nearly half (n=51, 46%) of defendants charged with battery were accommodated by the scheme.

[21] In Hull under a fifth (n=17, 17%) of accommodated defendants were assessed as having suitable accommodation compared with two thirds (n=34, 67%) in Scarborough.

[22] Thirty-five cases were supervised in a different area to where the court granting bail was situated. York magistrates' court was the largest exporter of cases transferring 12 cases to other areas.

[23] There were some gaps in the accommodation data caused largely by a change in personnel during the pilot period so full accommodation records are not available for all defendants.

24 Defendants in Hull spent substantially longer (a mean time of 98 days) in EBS accommodation compared with other areas (67 days in Sheffield, 64 days in Leeds, 56 days in York, 43 days in Bradford and Sheffield and 12 days in HSN).

25 The mean time spent in EBS accommodation after bail support had ended was 49 days ranging from 1 to 269 days. Two-thirds (n=55, 65%) of these defendants stayed in EBS accommodation for over two weeks.

26 The oldest mean age of defendants was in Sheffield (29 years) while the youngest mean age was in Bradford (26 years).

27 Sheffield and Hull had the highest proportion of women on the scheme (n=18, 12% and n=13, 11% respectively) whereas Bradford (n=9), Leeds (n=12) and York (n=4) had between 7 and 9% women, Scarborough 6% and HSN zero.

28 The comparable figure for men was three-quarters (n=158, 77%).

29 For example, numbers are small but slightly more BME defendants whose EBS proposals were rejected by the courts were charged with more serious violence offences than white defendants (32% (n=12) compared with 24% (n=45)).

30 In two-fifths (n=30, 44%) of the cases involving BME defendants where EBS was not proposed defendants were remanded in custody. Half of this group were bailed (n=34, 50%).

31 In three-fifths (n=23, 61%) of cases involving BME defendants in which proposal for EBS were made, defendants were remanded in custody with a third (n=12, 32%) being conditional bailed.

32 Proposals to offer EBS and RoB simultaneously are likely to have a limited impact for BME defendants as only three of the 47 BME defendants remanded in custody, who were assessed as being ineligible for EBS, were recorded as being eligible for RoB.

33 Nearly half (n=317, 49%) of defendants on the EBS were facing single charges. A further quarter (n=170, 26%) were charged with two offences. The highest number of charges faced by a defendant was nine. There was some variation between areas. The proportion of defendants facing a single charge varied from 45% in Sheffield to 55% in York.

34 HSN was not included because of the small number of defendants who had been on the scheme.

35 Only the most commonly charged offences are shown and only when large differences are apparent between areas.

36 Including MG4 (charge notice) and MG7 (police remand recommendation).

37 The EBS group had slightly less lengthy criminal histories, were less likely to have served a custodial sentence, were less likely to be on bail at the time of the offence, were less likely to have a record of offending on bail, failing to appear and breaching bail.

The Effective Bail Scheme's work with defendants

This chapter explores the work of the EBS. It first discusses the assessment process before going on to examine the work undertaken by the EBS while defendants were on the scheme including the provision of support through mentoring. It primarily draws on data collated from bail support files with mentoring information being collected from records compiled by SOVA.

Identifying needs

All defendants should have had their needs assessed while on the EBS. Two assessment tools were used: a needs assessment which should have been completed for all defendants and a housing assessment[1] completed for those with identified housing needs. The majority of defendants (n=585, 89%) had their needs assessed by one or both of these tools.[2] Over two-fifths (n=290, 44%) of defendants had both needs and housing assessments completed which involved some duplication of resources. There was also evidence that defendants' needs were sometimes missed and discrepancies existed between the two types of assessments, suggesting that they could be rationalised into one assessment tool.[3] This would ensure also that all the needs of defendants are assessed. This is important because in nearly a fifth (n=103, 16%) of cases in which an accommodation need was identified during a needs assessment no housing assessment was undertaken.

Most defendants on the EBS were identified as having a wide range of needs. Their identified needs were typical of offender populations (SEU, 2002). In terms of drug use, in just over two-fifths (278, 42%) of cases defendants were identified as having drug issues. This raises questions about the efficiency of the Drug Interventions Programme (DIP) generally but particularly RoB which should have resulted in very few drug using defendants being on the EBS (see Hucklesby et al, 2007). Most (n=245) of the defendants who disclosed using drugs were picked up during the needs assessment process but a small number were not (n=33).

In 215 cases defendants identified themselves as current drug users with a further 41 defendants disclosing prescribed methadone use only. Table 5.1 shows the most harmful drug used at the time assessments took place. Over three-fifths of this group (n=132, 64%) disclosed using a single drug. Nearly all of the heroin and crack/cocaine use was daily or two or three times a week and would indicate problematic use. Thirty-two of the cannabis users also reported using daily.

Table 5.1 Most 'harmful' drug used by defendants at the time of EBS assessment

Drug	Number
Cannabis	127
Heroin	37
Crack and/or cocaine	27
Amphetamines	15
Ecstasy	5
Tranquillisers	3
Total	**214**

Previous drug use was disclosed in a further 142 cases. Nearly two-fifths (n=55, 39%) of these defendants were previous users of heroin with a further quarter disclosing previous use of crack (n=23) and/or cocaine (n=17). In 100 cases drug use was reported to be linked to offending.[4] A substantial minority of defendants on the EBS had current or past issues with drug use which highlights the need to work closely with the DIP as well as the potential for EBS and RoB conditions to be imposed simultaneously.

Alcohol clearly played a part in many defendants' lives. Alcohol was identified as an issue in over half of cases (n=371, 57%) and a problem in 278 of these. In 144 cases, alcohol use was reported to be linked with offending. This was supported by data from the police which highlighted that nearly a fifth (n=111, 17%) of alleged offences were alcohol related. In a third (n=94, 34%) of cases defendants disclosed using alcohol daily. The majority of interviewees reported using large quantities of alcohol in a typical session. Many defendants were not receiving assistance with their alcohol use.

Details of employment histories and income were only available from needs assessments. Just over a quarter (n=133, 25%) of defendants were working (n=70), were unable to work because of ill-health (n=38) or were attending training or undertaking voluntary work (n=25). Two-thirds (n=234, 40%) of defendants were identified as unemployed. In terms of education, 79 (14%) defendants were identified as having no educational qualifications. Nearly three-quarters (n=378, 72%) of defendants identified problematic relationships with families or friends.

In most cases (n=385, 71%), defendants relied on benefits for their income. Thirty-six defendants stated that they had no income. Most defendants (n=164, 82%) relied on incomes of less than £100 per week. Debts were discussed as part of both needs and housing assessments. Levels of debt were also high with over half of the defendants (n=303, 52%) who were assessed stating that they were in debt. Half (n=75, 51%) of these defendants had debts of over £500.

In over two-fifths (n=252, 43%) of cases, defendants were identified as having mental health problems. In nearly two-fifths (n=97, 38%) of these cases, defendants were assessed as being at risk of suicide or self harm and in nearly half (n=121, 48%) of the cases, defendants were identified as suffering from depression. In addition, in nearly half (n=117, 46%) of the cases, defendants identified health concerns.

Three-fifths (n=354, 61%) of defendants had accommodation needs identified.[5] Most related to bail conditions which required them to reside at a particular address (n=238, 67%) but others suggested that defendants had no permanent accommodation or were living in unsuitable accommodation (n=57, 16%). Nowhere in the files was it recorded explicitly whether defendants required accommodation after their bail episode was completed. It cannot be assumed that all defendants who were housed by the scheme would have accommodation needs afterwards because their permanent accommodation may be unsuitable for bail purposes or that defendants who were not accommodated had no housing needs. It is important, therefore, for bail support schemes to enquire and record defendants long-term housing status particularly as lack of suitable housing is linked to an increased likelihood of offending (SEU, 2002).

In just over half (n=319, 54%) of cases in which assessments were completed, it was recorded that defendants were already in touch with other agencies at the time the assessment took place. They were recorded as being in contact with a wide range of agencies, most commonly, the Probation Service (n=211, 66%), the DIP or drugs agency (n=82, 26%), social services (n=26, 8%) and Youth Offending Teams (n=24, 8%). This indicates the potential for duplication of resources and over-burdening defendants with requirements but also presents an opportunity to work in collaboration with other organisations.

Dealing with defendants' needs

The first stage of dealing with defendants' needs was to draw up support plans. Three-fifths (n=432, 61%) of files contained support plans which had been completed. The rate of completion varied between areas with Scarborough and Sheffield having the highest completion rates (87% and 80% respectively). Bradford (49%), Hull (50%) and York (56%) had the lowest completion rates of support plans. The patchy use of support plans raises issues about whether the assistance provided by the EBS was focused accurately. The timing of completion of support plans also raises concerns. Only three-fifths (n=272, 63%) of support plans were completed within two weeks of the imposition of bail support.

The average number of needs identified in support plans was 2.6, although the highest number of needs identified in any one file was seven. Table 5.2 provides details of the needs identified in support plans. The range of needs was relatively narrow focusing on education, employment and training (ETE) (n=230, 61%) housing (n=226, 60%), and benefits and finance (n=132, 31%). Patterns in relation to the most common needs were identified between areas which may suggest that defendants in different areas had different needs, or it could indicate a formulaic approach to completing support plans. Most files suggested that needs would be worked on through referrals to relevant agencies. However, they indicated that a substantial minority of needs would be worked on within the project by bail accommodation officers (n=182), bail support officers (n=177) or SOVA (n=160).

Table 5.2 Needs identified in support plans

	Number	Percentage of cases in which support needs were recorded (n=379)[6]
ETE	230	61
Housing	226	60
Benefits/money	132	35
Alcohol	101	27
Lifestyle	99	26
Drugs	71	19
Mental health	57	15
Health	35	9
Anger	35	9
Other	69	18
Total	**1,055**	

Assessing risk

When working with defendants it is good practice to assess the risks posed to workers, the public and defendants. During the interviews, EBS staff raised concerns about the procedures for assessing risks within the project, citing a lack of guidance and training. Data confirm that there was potential for risk issues to be missed.[7] Differences existed between areas as to whether risk screening and/or assessments were completed, which may have been linked to different caseloads in the areas.[8] In only two-thirds (n=247, 66%) of cases was risk screening undertaken during the first week that defendants were on the EBS which potentially puts staff at risk. There was also evidence that some risk screening was carried out well into bail periods, with 36 risk screening documents being completed over a month after periods of EBS begun.

Three-fifths (n=397, 61%) of cases involved defendants who raised risk concerns for workers. Nearly three-quarters (n=282, 71%) of these defendants had full risk assessments undertaken with a partial risk assessment being completed in a further 16 cases.[9] Table 5.3 provides details of the areas which caused concerns for workers. It demonstrates that violence was the most commonly identified risk although relationships, suicide and self-harm and alcohol were identified as risk factors in around a third of cases.

Defendants were classified by the EBS in terms of risk in four areas – risk to children, adults, the public and staff. The highest risk category in the first three areas was calculated. Using this measure, a quarter (n=163, 25%) of defendants were categorised as medium risk in at least one area. Under a tenth (n=53, 8%) of defendants were categorised as low risk. Six per cent (n=37) of defendants were categorised in at least one area as high or very high risk. Levels of risk were fairly evenly distributed between areas. In addition, 29 defendants were assessed to be a medium or high risk to staff.

Table 5.3 Risks identified in case files

	Number	Percentage of cases in which risks were identified (n=397)
Violence	374	94
Relationships	149	38
Suicide/self-harm	147	37
Alcohol	131	33
Previous convictions	91	23
Mental health	86	22
Weapon	78	20
Vulnerability	80	20
Substance use	70	18
Current offence	42	11
Risk to Children	43	11
Escalating gravity of offending	41	10
Sexual offence	23	6
Risk to women	7	2
Other	27	7

Supervising defendants

Scheduled contacts

Defendants on the EBS were required to attend three appointments per week. The intensity of the contacts between defendants and the EBS was one of its selling points and in theory demarcated it from the Bail Accommodation and Support Scheme (BASS).[10] However, there were different interpretations of what constituted a contact. For the scheme, contacts included appointments with other agencies, telephone contacts as well as face-to-face meetings with defendants. By contrast some remand decision-makers assumed that all contacts were with EBS staff resulting in a mismatch between expectations and delivery. The remainder of this section discusses the contacts between the EBS and defendants.

Defendants were provided with weekly plans by staff, which gave details of the appointments which they were required to attend each week. Most files (n=593, 91%) included at least some weekly plans and over half of these (n=336, 57%) included plans for every week that defendants were on the EBS. The rest had some missing weekly plans. The total number of weekly plans available was 4,948. The majority (n=4,920, 83%) of weekly plans indicated that defendants would have contact with the scheme on three or more occasions in a week. Nearly a fifth (n=853, 17%)

of weekly plans suggested that less than three contacts per week were planned. Compliance with the scheme's policy of three contacts a week varied between areas and this was not linked to differences in caseloads. In two areas (Bradford, 71% and York, 75%) only three-quarters of weekly plans indicated that three meetings per week were planned. In other areas (Leeds and HSN) compliance was higher than average (88% and 89% respectively).

Table 5.4 provides details of the meetings which were scheduled. Three-fifths (n=9007, 61%) of the planned meetings were scheduled to take place in EBS offices with project staff. A further 13% of meetings would take place with EBS staff in defendants' accommodation. Over a tenth (n=1878, 13%) of planned contacts were by telephone. Notable, was the relatively small number of planned contacts with mentors (n=957, 7%) which is discussed further below. Over a tenth (n=1884, 13%) of scheduled contacts were with agencies outside the EBS.

There were substantial differences between areas in the types of meetings which were scheduled. The number of meetings with scheme staff at the EBS offices ranged from three-quarters (n=1902, 76%) in Hull to (n=2412, 52%) in Leeds and (n=130, 49%) in HSN. The use of home visits varied from a nearly a fifth (n=57, 21%) in HSN to under a tenth in Scarborough (n=54, 5%). Planned use of telephone contacts varied between a fifth (n=696, 20%) of contacts in Sheffield to under 5% in Hull (n=117, 5%), Scarborough (n=40, 4%) and York (n=44, 5%). The use of appointments with other agencies as EBS contacts differed also. They constituted under a fifth (n=168, 16%) of all planned meetings in Scarborough compared with 5% in Sheffield (n=186) and 2% in Bradford (n=38). Some of the variation may be explained by differences in the circumstances of defendants or by the area covered (for example whether the area was rural or urban). However, defendants' obligations in terms of complying with the scheme, to some extent, depended on which area they happened to be supervised by. This has the potential to cause injustice. Remand decision-makers may also feel misinformed about the nature of contacts.

Table 5.4 Details of scheduled meetings with defendants

	Number	Percentage of total number of contacts
Office meetings	9007	61
Telephone contacts	1878	13
Home visits	1897	13
SOVA	957	7
Probation	306	2
Substance use agencies	103	1
ETE	102	1
Mental health agency	44	>1
Foundation Housing	38	>1
Other agencies	371	3
Total	**14,703**	**100**

Contacts between EBS staff and defendants

Meetings

After every contact with defendants, project workers were required to complete a contact sheet providing details of what was discussed and so on. This was important not only to record the work of the project but also to keep track of what happened in individual cases. In most cases (n=618, 94%) files contained contacts sheets although some were incomplete.[11]

The number of contacts with defendants was obviously dependant on the length of time that defendants were on the scheme. However, it also provides information about workload. The number of contacts logged for individuals ranged from 1 to 107. The total amount of contact time for individual cases ranged from five minutes to 44 hours. The mean contact time for individual meetings was just under half an hour (27 minutes) and ranged from three minutes to nearly three hours (165 minutes). Differences existed between areas, with the mean time spent on cases in different areas ranging from just over four hours in Sheffield to over eight hours in York and over 10 hours in HSN. The mean time spent per meeting also differed between areas and ranged from 22 minutes in Leeds to 40 minutes in York and HSN.

Details of 12,141 contacts were available which provides a clear picture of the nature of contacts between EBS staff and defendants. Contacts between staff and defendants took a variety of forms. Most commonly, contacts took place in EBS offices (n=7392, 61%) although home visits (n=2262, 19%) and face-to-face contacts in other locations (n=146, 1%) also took place. A fifth (n=2309, 19%) of contacts between staff and defendants were made by telephone. The proportion of contacts by different methods varied between areas, sometimes reflecting the nature of the area covered, for example HSN (a large rural area) made lower use of face-to-face meetings and more use of telephone contacts. The proportion of face-to-face meetings which took place in EBS offices ranged from nearly four-fifths (n=916, 79%) in Scarborough to around a half in HSN[12] (n=101, 49%) and York (n=471, 56%). The number of home visits also varied from a quarter (n=692, 25%) in Leeds to just 2% in Bradford. The substitution of telephone calls for face-to-face contacts was used as a way of managing caseloads, so it would be expected that areas with the highest caseloads would have the highest proportion of contacts made by telephone. However, this was not the pattern which emerged. The greatest use of telephone calls was in HSN (n=55, 27%), Sheffield (n=727, 26%) and Bradford (n=392, 22%). The lowest use of telephones was in Scarborough (n=129, 11%), Hull (n=339, 13%) and Leeds (n=473, 17%). There were widely divergent practices used in areas in relation to the nature of contacts with defendants. While some of this may be explained by local circumstances such as staffing issues, differences in caseloads, the geographical demands of HSN and so on, it appears not to explain all of the variation. As a consequence, defendants had different demands placed upon them during their time on the scheme.

The majority (n=9875, 83%) of recorded contacts were between defendants and bail support officers. Relatively few meetings (n=1708, 14%) were between defendants and bail accommodation officers. This may reflect reality although it is also possible that bail accommodation officers were less likely to record their contacts with defendants because they usually took place away from EBS offices.

All defendants had an initial meeting with EBS workers which involved signing paperwork and explaining the scheme. Table 5.5 provides details of the issues which were recorded as being discussed at subsequent meetings. A wide range of issues were discussed during meetings. In over a quarter (n=4430, 27%) of meetings discussion was general in nature, most often checking that everything was alright. Housing (n=2275, 14%) and legal/court issues (n=2004, 12%) were the next most commonly discussed issues.

Table 5.5 Issues discussed during meetings between defendants and EBS staff

	Number	Percentage
General update/support	4,430	27
Housing	2,275	14
Legal/court issues	2,004	12
Education, employment and training (ETE)	1,351	8
Benefits	1,031	8
Child/family/relations	696	4
Alcohol	670	4
Health	538	3
Compliance issues	462	3
Drugs	461	3
Assessment	437	3
Mental health	432	3
Lifestyle	400	2
Debt/fines	249	2
Bail support accommodation	215	1
Current alleged offending	184	1
Provide clothing/food	159	1
Mentoring	123	1
Other	253	2
Total	**16,370**	**100**

Contact sheets also recorded whether defendants attended planned meetings. Three-quarters (n=9237, 78%) of contacts were recorded as being kept by defendants with a further tenth (n=1358, 12%) being non-statutory contacts where compliance was not required. Defendants were recorded as missing nearly a tenth (n=937, 8%) of meetings. In two-fifths (n=381, 41%) of cases acceptable reasons were provided by defendants. In 235 cases, defendants were either late for meetings or were drunk.

Other direct contacts with defendants

EBS staff were also in contact with defendants by letter and telephone. Letters were sent to defendants in 143 cases, mostly to inform them about appointments (n=111). Telephone contacts with defendants were much more frequent (n=382, 58%). The mean number of telephone calls made per case was 5.7 and the number ranged from 1 to 35. Telephone calls were usually made to rearrange (n=94) or chase missed (n=94) appointments or remind or confirm appointments with defendants (n=52). Defendants also contacted staff to inform them that they were unable to attend appointments (n=49). Other reasons for telephone calls taking place were because they were statutory appointments (n=232),[13] to provide general updates (n=191) or give advice to defendants (n=32).

Indirect work on cases

It was recorded on files when work was carried out on cases which did not involve direct contact with defendants, for example, referring defendants to other agencies. Indirect contacts were recorded in four-fifths (n=511, 78%) of cases. The average number of indirect contacts per case was 9.46 and ranged from 1 to 57. This suggests that project workers were actively referring and liaising with other agencies. However, there were wide discrepancies in the mean number of indirect contacts per area with the mean number being considerably lower in Bradford (5.45 per case) than the other areas where contacts ranged from 9.51 in Leeds to 14.70 in HSN. The majority of indirect contacts were by telephone (n=501), but written forms of communication (n=474) were also used.

Table 5.6 provides details of which agencies EBS was contacting in relation to defendants. They contacted a wide range of agencies, organisations and individuals. Most commonly they contacted accommodation providers, the Probation Service and the police. Notably only 37 of the probation contacts were recorded as being with Pre-Sentence Report authors, suggesting that little liaison was taking place in relation to feeding information about compliance with bail support into the sentencing process. This is a potential gap in the EBS. Compliance with the EBS may signal an increased likelihood of compliance with non-custodial sentences and providing such information to those passing sentences has the potential to reduce the use of custodial sentences.

The majority of contacts were recorded as being to either confirm details about defendants (n=1596, 32%), for general updates (n=1347, 27%) or to receive or give advice or discuss concerns (n=429, 9%). A small but significant number of indirect contacts related to defendants' non-compliance (n=286, 6%) or checking up on their compliance (n=114, 2%). A further 12% (n=614) of contacts were recorded as making referrals to or appointments with other agencies.

Table 5.6 Agencies contacted by EBS staff

	Number	Percentage
Accommodation provider inc Foundation Housing	670	13
Probation	619	12
Police	511	10
SOVA	385	8
Other EBS staff	363	7
Solicitor	350	7
Court	332	7
Family/partner	248	5
Benefits office	233	5
Foundation Housing	212	4
ETE institution	187	4
Drugs Intervention Programme/drugs agencies	163	3
G4S	158	3
Social services	95	2
Mental health professionals	76	2
Alcohol agency	75	2
Charitable organisation	40	1
Other	258	5
Total	**4,975**	**100**

Feedback and feed-in to the courts

Providing feedback to the courts on the EBS gives it credibility. This was one of the functions of the Local Advisory Groups. On an individual case level, EBS staff were supposed to supply regular progress reports to courts during the time that defendants were subject to bail support. In theory, they also provided final reports which would feed in to the sentencing process. The files suggest that the reality was different. At least one progress report was present in defendants' files in just over a third (n=242, 37%) of cases. The presence and number of progress reports varied between areas.[14] A similar picture emerged in relation to final reports. Around one fifth (n=111, 17%) of files contained final reports and completion varied between areas, with around a third (n=25, 36%) of files in Scarborough containing final reports compared with a tenth (n=14, 9%) in Leeds. Feedback was routinely provided to the court only when defendants appeared in court for breaching bail support. In these circumstances, the information provided ranged from a full report to a note stating whether the EBS would accept the defendant back onto the scheme. Similar information was not usually available when defendants were accused of breaching other bail conditions or of another offence partly because the EBS were often not aware that defendants were appearing in court.

Progress and final reports were not being routinely provided to courts and some areas had a culture of producing reports whereas others did not. This may be explained by the expectations of the courts or staff's unwillingness to provide negative information to courts which may result in defendants leaving the scheme and/or being remanded in custody. Indeed, most (n=160, 84%) progress reports were positive. However, progress reports feed into the sentencing process, build confidence in the scheme and provide feedback to courts. Those making decisions about remand commented generally on the lack of feedback about the EBS, particularly in individual cases.

A second way in which feedback can be provided to the courts and potentially have an impact on sentencing decisions is for compliance with bail support to feed into reports prepared by the Probation Service for sentencing. This requires liaison between bail support teams and report writers. Most project officers reported that they contacted report authors but some did this more frequently than others. There was only limited evidence of the process in defendants' files, in completed reports and through interviews with criminal justice professionals although verbal rather than written communication was reported to be the norm. This raises a more general issue about liaison between the EBS and the probation services. There was a willingness on the part of both the EBS and the Probation Service to increase liaison particularly at the management level. Competing commitments and resourcing issues particularly within the Probation Service hampered progress. Resistance to voluntary sector organisations running such schemes was voiced by some probation staff echoing previous research (see Chapter One). Some probation staff viewed bail information and bail support as a role they could provide more robustly and cheaply, which is an interesting perspective given the resistance of the Probation Service historically to become involved in pre-trial work (see Chapter One).

Mentoring

Mentoring support was provided by volunteers and was an integral part of the EBS. Theoretically, all defendants on the scheme were supposed to be referred for mentoring support but there was disagreement about how mentors fitted into the scheme. It was anticipated originally that mentors would be used to help manage the caseload of the scheme but in fact their purpose was blurred. It was unclear whether mentors were to be used as a supplement or a substitute for statutory appointments with paid staff. In reality they were used more often to supplement statutory meetings, providing additional support to defendants, but this varied between areas (see Hucklesby et al, 2008). Interviewees generally recognised that mentors played an important part in the scheme and added value. Most EBS staff provided examples of when mentoring had worked well, but the role they undertook varied between areas.

The amount of time required to implement a volunteer mentoring scheme was underestimated. This is demonstrated by Figures 5.1 and 5.2 which show that mentoring was slow to take off. By the end of 2007 both commencements and caseloads were rising. However, by April 2008 commencements had tailed off and caseloads began to decline. Over four-fifths (n=544, 83%) of defendants were recorded as being referred to SOVA for mentoring support. Over half (n=309, 57%)

of these defendants were known not to have been matched with a mentor. In a third (n=104, 34%) of cases no reasons were recorded for a mentor match not taking place. Reasons provided in other cases included that a mentor was not required (n=46), the case had been closed (n=55), that defendants were assessed as having no needs (n=29), the defendant had been breached (n=28) or been remanded in

Figure 5.1 Mentoring commencement

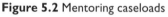

Figure 5.2 Mentoring caseloads

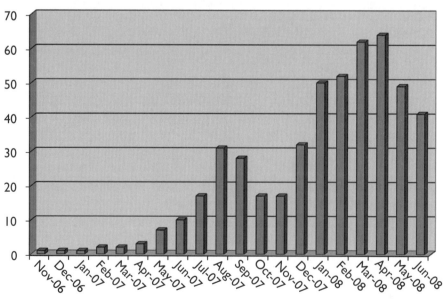

custody (n=21) before a match could take place. In 17 cases defendants were deemed to be too high risk to be matched with mentors. It was recorded that 235 defendants were matched with mentors. Four-fifths (n=188, 80%) met with mentors and a further tenth (n=27, 17%) had contact with mentors by telephone only. A total of 20 defendants were known not to have had contact with mentors.[15] In nine of these cases it was clear that appointments had been arranged but had not taken place.

A third (n=215, 33%) of the total number of defendants on the scheme had contact with mentors. The mean duration of contact between mentors and defendants was 42 days and the longest contact was around nine months. In terms of contact between mentors and defendants, the mean number of contacts which were arranged was 5.88 and ranged from 1 to 45. The total number of sessions which actually took place was lower (5.07 per defendants ranging from 1 to 44). The picture which emerged was that a relatively small number of defendants had regular and sustained contact with mentors, with a significant minority (n=69, 32%) of cases where defendants had contact with a mentor on more than five occasions. However, just under two-fifths (n=83, 39%) of defendants had contact with a mentor on only one or two occasions resulting in a significant proportion of defendants having much more limited contact with mentors.

The majority of the work undertaken by mentors took the form of face-to-face meetings with defendants (n=783).[16] Contact by telephone was less frequent (n=288).[17] In 35 cases, defendants received home visits from mentors.[18] Mentors undertaking home visits raise risk concerns and it was not clear that adequate safeguards had been put in place to ensure their safety.

Details of the issues recorded as being discussed between mentors and defendants throughout the lifetime of a case can be found in Table 5.7. The issues discussed during mentoring sessions were similar to those discussed in statutory appointments with paid staff raising issues of potential overlap. A wide range of issues were discussed during mentoring contacts but most frequently discussions were of a general nature followed by legal/court issues and finance, benefit and debt. Mentors also provided practical assistance and advice such as completing curriculum vitae, providing information about education and training courses and attending court appearances, but these activities were recorded much less often.[19] In 35 cases it was recorded that mentors had referred defendants onto a wide range of other agencies including statutory and voluntary services.

The total amount of time mentors spent on cases ranged from five minutes to 140 hours. The mean time spent on a case was just over nine hours. This time was divided between time spent with defendants (direct time), on tasks related to individual cases such as travelling to appointments (indirect time) and on other activities such as shadowing workers. Direct time spent with defendants accounted for two-fifths (n=50,297 minutes, 41%) of total mentoring time.[20] Mentoring activities were concentrated on relatively few individuals: just under two-thirds (n=137, 64%) of defendants spent two hours or less with mentors with half of this group (n=80) spending an hour or less with mentors. Meetings lasted for an average of just over 30 minutes and ranged from only a few minutes to three hours.[21] Slightly less time was spent dealing indirectly with defendants' cases[22] which accounted for a fifth (n=25,005 minutes, 20%) of total mentor time. Nearly two-fifths (n=48,360 minutes, 39%) of mentor time involved non-case related activities such as training and shadowing EBS staff.[23] While including this in calculations about mentoring activities is important for matched funding purposes, it gives the impression that a higher level of contact between defendants and mentors was taking place than was the reality.

Table 5.7 Issues discussed per case between mentors and defendants[24]

	Number
General information	170
Legal/court issues	96
Finance, benefit and debt	89
Employment	79
Housing	76
Personal/family matters	68
Education and training	63
Lifestyle	63
Health	56
Alcohol use	43
Basic needs	20
Drug use	17
Total	**840**

A relatively high number of planned meetings between mentors and defendants did not take place. This may reflect the fact that these meetings were generally not statutory appointments so that defendants would not be returned to court for non-compliance if they did not attend. Over half (n=104, 55%) of defendants missed at least one appointment with their mentors.[25] On 126 occasions, no reason was provided by defendants for missing appointments. Given the extent of missed appointments and the central role of mentoring within the EBS consideration should be given to whether appropriate sanctions are available for non-compliance.

Mentors were recorded as missing appointments on 33 occasions and in nine cases this included multiple appointments for the same case suggesting that the EBS was slow to respond to problems which arose in a small number of cases. However, their options for dealing with such problems are limited when dealing with volunteers rather than paid workers (see Hucklesby and Worrall, 2007).

In over a third (n=79, 37%) of cases mentoring contact finished when defendants left the EBS. In 12 cases mentoring contacts continued after defendants had completed their bail period. In over half (n=123, 57%) of cases mentoring contact finished before the end of the period on EBS.

This chapter has examined the work carried out by the EBS as recorded in the case files and discussed in interviews. The next chapter explores stakeholders' and defendants' perspectives on the scheme.

Notes

[1] Housing assessments had a narrower focus than needs assessments concentrating on issues which may have an impact on defendants' ability to be accepted into housing. These included rent arrears (n=32), areas from where defendants were banned (n=83), current Anti-Social Behaviour Orders (n=15), cultural needs (n=6) and their alleged offences or convictions including arson (n=15), sexual offences (n=11), racially motivated offences (n=8) and violence (n=165).

[2] A further two-fifths of defendants (n=268, 41%) had only a needs assessment completed and 27 defendants had a housing assessment completed but no needs assessment. A tenth of defendants (n=70, 11%) had neither their general nor housing needs assessed.

[3] For example, 33 defendants disclosed using drugs during their needs assessment but not during their housing assessment.

[4] The cases were spread across all courts.

[5] A total of 282 files contained housing assessments. In 218 of these cases, accommodation needs were also identified during needs assessments.

[6] 53 support plans contained no details of support needs.

[7] A quarter (n= 173, 26%) of files contained no risk information. A further fifth (n=141, 22%) of files contained the risk screening document used for initial assessments by Bail Support Officers. Just under half (n=318, 49%) of the files contained a completed risk assessment although some of these (n=21) were only partially completed.

[8] The highest number of risk screening/assessments were completed in Scarborough (n=62, 93%) while the lowest proportion of risk assessments were completed in Leeds (n=73, 46%). The rest of the areas completed risk screening/assessments in between 71% and 83% of cases.

[9] Most of the remaining cases had risk screening completed (n=94).

[10] BASS contact sessions are reduced from three to one per week after the first three weeks, with two sessions in the weeks before and (if accommodated and not remanded in custody) after trial.

[11] Thirty-seven files contained no contact sheets.

[12] The lower use of face-to-face meetings and the higher rate of telephone use in HSN reflects the nature of supervising defendants over a wide geographic rural area.

[13] The EBS made a policy decision during the pilot period that some contacts could be made by telephone rather than face-to-face. Telephone calls made for this purpose were recorded as statutory appointments.

[14] The number of files containing at least one progress report varied between areas. Over half of files in Hull (56%), Scarborough (61%) and Sheffield (50%) contained progress reports compared with less than a third in Bradford (29%) and York (28%) and less than a tenth (6%) in Leeds. The number of progress reports in each file ranged from one to five. Leeds only ever produced one progress report per case whereas Hull regularly produced more than one.

[15] Four defendants had left the EBS before mentoring could be arranged.

[16] The mean number of face-to-face meetings per case was 4.51 and ranged from one to 30.

[17] The mean number of telephone contacts between mentors and defendants was 3.82 per case.

[18] The number of home visits per case ranged from one to seven and the mean number of visits was 1.97.

[19] For example, in 23 cases it was recorded that education/training material was provided to defendants and in four cases it was recorded that the mentor had assisted defendants with their CVs.

[20] The mean time spent directly with defendants per case was just under four hours and ranged from five minutes to nearly 17 hours.

[21] SOVA required mentors to record time spent on cases in 15-minute blocks.

[22] A mean time of 2 hours and 24 minutes ranging between 15 minutes to 21 hours.

[23] The mean time spent on these activities was nearly four hours and ranged from 15 minutes to over 55 hours.

[24] These issues may have been discussed on more than one occasion.

[25] Most defendants missed one appointment only (n=59) although 20 defendants missed three or more appointments.

6

Interviewees' perspectives on the Effective Bail Scheme

This chapter focuses on interviewees' views about the EBS. It draws on interviews with stakeholders, workers and defendants which took place in the early stages of the pilot. The interviews reflect the position at a time when the EBS was still being implemented and after which changes were made in order to improve its operation. Nevertheless, interviewees' views were generally positive, supporting the establishment of the EBS.

Stakeholders' and workers' perspectives

Most interviewees viewed the implementation of the scheme as a success at the time they were interviewed. The views of those closely involved in the scheme were summed up by one interviewee who commented: "It is set up, it is running and it has got the sort of caseload that we hoped … and it has done so without any negative comments." At this stage, success was viewed in terms of implementing and operating the scheme and reaching target numbers. Interviewees viewed the considerable time and effort put into the development of the scheme prior to implementation as crucial to its success along with the phased introduction of the scheme across the courts. Interviewees also noted that accommodation had been sourced and that more defendants than planned had been accommodated with low levels of damage to property and very few major incidents.[1] Indeed, most interviewees reported that compliance with the scheme was higher than they had expected. The fact that most interviewees had received no complaints or negative feedback about the scheme was also viewed as an indicator of success. As one interviewee noted, "silence is a good sign".

Most criminal justice professionals[2] welcomed the introduction of the scheme. Unsurprisingly, given its presence in the courts, they were more knowledgeable about the BIP than the EBS. The main benefit of bail information schemes was viewed as the provision of independent, accurate and objective information. It was also viewed as saving both court and criminal justice professionals' time because it speeded up the process by verifying information such as defendants' addresses, sentence status and compliance with other court orders and licence conditions. Interviewees welcomed bail information reports because they increased the availability of information, which gave decision-makers more confidence in their decisions. However, responses of criminal justice professionals to the scheme varied between areas. Most notably, in one area, the scheme was not well received by members of the CPS. They generally saw no need for the scheme, although they acknowledged that it was useful because it could find accommodation for defendants. They also did not see a role for bail information because they relied on defence solicitors and the police to verify accommodation.

The CPS rarely raised the possibility of bail support conditions in court and they generally did not view this as their role. Both the CPS and bail information officers saw this as defence solicitors' role. However, interviewees including defence solicitors themselves suggested that defence solicitors could not be relied on because their receptiveness to the scheme varied, awareness was patchy and they were 'lukewarm' about the scheme. Magistrates and District Judges were also wary of the accuracy of information provided by defence solicitors, mirroring research findings (see for example, Hucklesby, 1997a).

The aims of the EBS related to increasing short-term compliance while defendants were on the scheme. While there may be an aspiration to have an impact on long-term compliance, that is, desistence from offending, this was not an explicit aim of the scheme nor should it have been when defendants were legally innocent. Nevertheless, interviewees were confused about the aims of the EBS, describing its focus on offending-related factors or as an opportunity to begin work on issues which would normally be the focus of post-sentence work. Several workers were disillusioned because of the lack of in-depth work with defendants aimed at rehabilitation and/or desistence. Similarly, several bail information officers grappled with the issue of defendants' needs. They suggested that in order for defendants to be offered bail support, they had to have needs which could be addressed by the scheme. This raised a dilemma for them as one officer explained:

> If they've got no needs whatsoever, then sometimes it's pointless. But ... can I justify remanding somebody in custody because they've no needs?

The majority of criminal justice professionals and remand decision-makers viewed bail support as a useful tool. They saw its purpose primarily in terms of the provision of accommodation particularly away from the original court area. Many of them referred to the scheme as a replacement for bail hostels which had generally ceased accommodating defendants because of their use for high-risk offenders. Often interviewees thought that the scheme accommodated defendants in bail hostels and appeared unaware that the scheme had its own accommodation. The importance of accommodation was linked by interviewees to the high number of defendants charged with violence offences, particularly domestic violence, who often could not return to their normal residence. Other benefits of the scheme expressed by interviewees were that it provided structure for defendants while they were on bail, addressed support needs, monitored defendants while on bail and provided reassurance to decision-makers. One District Judge referred to bail support as providing 'monitoring and a hand on a [defendant's] shoulder'. In North Yorkshire, access to drugs services was viewed as a key benefit of the scheme as Restriction on Bail (RoB) was unavailable in this area.[3] However, even in areas where RoB was available, chaotic drug users were often highlighted as a target group. Indeed, it was evident that interviewees were unclear about the distinction between bail support and RoB.

Confidence in the scheme was high among most criminal justice interviewees and they generally viewed it as a credible scheme. However, part of its credibility was based on interviewees linking the scheme to the Probation Service. Indeed, nearly all criminal justice interviewees thought that the scheme was operated by, or at least linked to, the Probation Service. Few of them appeared to be aware that Nacro ran the scheme. From the courts' perspective, the bail information component is the most visible part of the scheme which probably explains these findings. A small number of those who make decisions about remand questioned the quality of contacts between staff and defendants and the quality and experience of the staff working on the scheme.

Considerable effort was put into publicising the EBS prior to its implementation. This was viewed very positively by managers and stakeholders and was seen as contributing to the success of the scheme. Nonetheless, awareness of the EBS among some criminal justice professionals was limited generally and most of them had only a vague understanding of what it involved for defendants. This suggests that awareness-raising activities need to be on-going. As one legal advisor said, "As the months go by, it might drop off someone's radar". Awareness of the scheme among probation staff was reported to be low especially among offender managers. This is likely to have had an impact on the aspiration to link bail support outcomes with pre-sentence reports (PSRs) and subsequent sentencing decisions. There was some evidence of animosity on the part of probation staff towards the scheme, but there were also examples of good practice, particularly those concerning the relationships between bail information officers and probation court teams. This link was vital when more than one court was covered by a single bail information officer who relied regularly on probation court staff to hand over reports and so on.

In spite of a general lack of detailed knowledge of EBS among interviewees, most of them were aware of the main aims of the scheme. They generally viewed it as achieving some of its aims, although this was often qualified because of the lack of empirical evidence. Unsurprisingly, the most positive comments came from individuals involved in delivering the scheme. They generally believed that the scheme was diverting defendants from custody and reducing non-attendance rates at court hearings but thought that it was less likely that the scheme would be reducing rates of offending on bail. Criminal Justice professionals and Partnership Board members were more circumspect. Generally, they perceived that the scheme may have had a marginal effect on custodial remands rates but it was also likely to have resulted in net-widening whereby bail support is imposed as an additional condition for defendants who would have been bailed in any event rather than for defendants who would have been remanded in custody. The greatest impact was perceived to be on court attendance rates. Interviewees thought that offending on bail rates had been unaffected, but that breach rates were lower than they had expected.

Defendants' perspectives

A total of 44 defendants were interviewed about the EBS. Generally, defendants were positive about their time on bail support and viewed it as a good scheme. Indeed, the majority of defendants stated that they would go on the scheme again and recommend it to others. The most positive aspect of the scheme was reported to be the general help and support it provided. Defendants also mentioned that it offered somewhere to live, someone to talk to, structure to their lives, as well as training, education and employment opportunities, and the opportunity to change lifestyles. Most defendants thought that there was nothing negative about the scheme. Defendants explained:

> They've given me a chance to sort myself out. They've helped me so much. I don't know what I would have done without bail support.

> I don't think there is anything else they could help with. They've done all they can … They've been there for me. If I hadn't got bail support I don't think I would've got through this.

> Not at first [I didn't want to be on the scheme], thought it'll be a standard 'meet someone and go', but to be honest it's been a real support for me, especially in a place I don't know anyone.

Table 6.1 shows defendants' views on the impact of the EBS on their behaviour. It demonstrates that the majority of interviewees thought that the scheme had assisted them during their bail period to comply with bail, offend less and provided them with help and support. Defendants elaborated on the impact of the scheme on their behaviour:

> For me, it's kept me out of trouble and I've kept to my appointments

> I'm not offending anymore. It's opened my eyes and them giving me a boot in the right direction rather than committing crimes.

> It makes you behave a little better. If you do anything wrong you'll go down … it keeps you on your toes.

In terms of mentoring, half of the defendants interviewed said that they wanted a mentor. A total of 33 defendants recalled being offered a mentor and 23 defendants claimed to have been given a mentor. Nineteen defendants were still in touch with their mentors at the time of the interview. Just over half of the defendants with mentors had been in contact with them on five or fewer occasions. The number of contacts ranged from 1 to 18. Most contacts were face-to-face meetings, but several defendants claimed to have been contacted by telephone on a significant number of occasions. Most defendants reported meeting their mentors weekly and the most popular places for meetings were coffee shops. A wide range of issues were discussed during these meetings.

Table 6.1 Defendants' perspectives on the impact of the EBS

	Very much	To some extent	Not really	Not at all	Not relevant	Total
Assisted to comply with bail conditions	31	4	1	2	0	38
Assisted to comply with bail	27	6	1	1	0	35
Assisted to attend court	24	6	4	2	1	37
Reduced offending on bail	26	3	1	4	3	37
Less likely to offend in the future	22	4	2	3	6	37
Provided general help and support	31	4	1	1	0	37
Helped with problems	29	4	0	3	0	36

Twenty-three of the defendants interviewed claimed to have met with a mentor while they were on the EBS. Generally, they were positive about their mentors, describing them as good listeners, supportive, really nice and caring. They had provided general support and in some cases assistance with particular issues such as benefits, employment and training and housing. The majority of defendants said that mentoring relationships had met with their expectations. Defendants explained:

> ... I didn't think I needed one [a mentor] but he was good when I met him. It was good to talk to someone else.

> She does everything to help. She's gone out of her way to help. She's looking into volunteering work for me ... She's just helped me with everyday problems. She's just a good lass to talk to.

Fifteen defendants who were interviewed had had contact with mentors. Table 6.2 provides details of how mentoring was reported to have had an impact on their behaviour. It demonstrates that the majority of defendants thought that mentoring had influenced their compliance and offending while on bail positively. Its greatest reported influence was the general assistance and support it provided. By contrast, a few defendants mentioned poor relationships with mentors when they did not turn up for appointments or did not really help.

In terms of accommodation, 17 (39%) interviewees had been housed by the scheme. The majority were content to be living in bail support accommodation and most described it as good or OK. Positive aspects of the accommodation were that it provided a settled address, allowed defendants to have their own space and was peaceful. However, a significant minority of defendants reported being lonely and missing family and friends. Several defendants were unhappy about sharing accommodation.

Table 6.2 Defendants' perspectives on the impact of mentoring

	Very much	To some extent	Not really	Total
Assisted to comply with bail conditions	4	7	3	14
Assisted to comply with bail	6	4	5	15
Assisted to comply with bail support	6	5	4	15
Assisted to attend court	5	3	7	15
Reduced offending on bail	6	5	4	15
Less likely to offend in the future	6	5	4	15
Provided general help and support	10	5	0	15
Helped with problems	10	5	0	15

Table 6.3 shows defendants responses in relation to the impact of accommodation on their behaviour. It shows that the majority of defendants were positive about the accommodation provided and reported that it increased their compliance with bail conditions. Around half of the defendants viewed EBS accommodation as having an impact on their offending behaviour while on bail. Additionally, six defendants reported that EBS accommodation had facilitated lifestyles changes. Defendants elaborated:

It's helped me a lot. It helped me settle.

It's been brilliant, absolutely brilliant. There's nothing better than closing the door behind you and knowing you have somewhere to go.

Table 6.3 Defendants' views on the impact of EBS accommodation

	Very much	To some extent	Not really	Not at all	Total
Assisted to comply with bail conditions	12	3	0	1	16
Assisted to comply with bail	8	3	0	2	13
Assisted to comply with bail support	12	1	1	1	15
Assisted to attend court	9	1	0	4	14
Reduced offending on bail	7	3	1	4	15
Less likely to offend in the future	4	3	3	2	12
Helped with problems	10	3	1	1	15

This chapter examined the main findings of the interviews which suggested that both criminal justice professionals and defendants supported the scheme. In the next chapter, initial findings relating to outcomes are discussed.

Notes

[1] It was originally envisaged that a quarter of defendants on the scheme would be accommodated. In reality, over a third of defendants on the scheme have been accommodated to-date.

[2] This group includes District Judges, magistrates, Crown Prosecutors, legal advisors and defence solicitors.

[3] Restriction on Bail was operational in Bradford, Hull, Leeds and Sheffield.

Interim outcomes of the Effective Bail Scheme

7

The EBS had a number of aims including reducing the incidence of breaches of bail conditions, failure to appear for court hearings and offending on bail. This chapter examines findings in relation to these aims as well as in terms of compliance with bail support. It also explores the outcomes of bail support periods. Data were collated from bail support files so it only includes incidents known to the EBS and is likely to underestimate the non-compliance events. Just over half (n=354, 54%) of EBS cases ended when defendants were sentenced. In other cases, bail support periods were completed when defendants were breached (n=95, 27%), allegedly committed new offences (n=89, 13%), or because their bail was varied (n=79, 12%).

Two-fifths (n=267, 41%) of defendants were not known to have been breached or offended on bail while on the EBS. Three-fifths (n=388, 59%) of defendants either breached their bail conditions or were charged with an offence on bail. A tenth (n=34, 10%) of the group breached bail support, other conditions and had been charged with an offence committed while on bail while a fifth (n=74, 19%) had breached either bail support or other conditions and allegedly offended while on bail.[1] A tenth (n=36, 9%) of defendants on EBS had breached both bail support and other conditions, but were not known to have offended while on bail. The mean time to breach of bail conditions was around a month.[2] The mean time to alleged offending on bail was 42 days.[3]

Breaches of bail conditions

Half (n=328, 50%) of defendants were known to have breached their bail conditions. Nearly a quarter (n=70, 23%) of this group breached both bail support and other bail conditions. Nearly half (n=138, 46%) breached bail support only with a further third (n=95, 31%) breaching bail conditions other than bail support. The mean time to breach was similar for breaches of bail support at around one month.[4]

Breach of bail support

Nearly a third (n=208, 32%) of defendants were known to have breached bail support. The majority (n=157, 75%) breached it once.[5] Nearly all (n=255, 96%) breaches of bail support were for failing to attend appointments.[6] The outcome of the first breach was recorded in 192 cases. Just over a quarter (n=53, 28%) of defendants were remanded in custody. This is a slightly higher proportion than for breaches of other conditions which may suggest that breaches of bail support were treated more seriously than breaches of other conditions. However, a significant minority of defendants were re-bailed with (n=79, 41%) or without (n=20, 10%) bail support conditions or no action was taken (n=13, 7%), perhaps suggesting that bail support was not being used as an alternative to custodial remands.[7] Conversely, it may be that courts were willing to give defendants one further chance to comply with bail support before using custodial remands. However, this strategy does not appear to have been adopted by the courts. Only a fifth (n=9, 19%) of defendants were remanded in custody as a result of a second breach of bail support with over two-fifths (n=21, 44%) being re-bailed to the scheme and a tenth (n=5, 10%) being re-bailed without bail support conditions. After the third breach, the majority (five out eight) of defendants were re-bailed and three defendants were remanded in custody.[8] These data suggest that bail support was not routinely being used as an alternative to custodial remands. The reluctance of remand decision-makers to use custodial remands as a penalty for breach may also indicate that a degree of net-widening occurred.

Breach of other bail conditions

A fifth (n=146, 23%) of defendants were known to have breached other bail conditions. This is likely to be an underestimate of the breach rate because the EBS would not necessarily be aware of breaches of other bail conditions and no schematic procedure existed to record these data (see Hucklesby et al, 2008). The number of breaches ranged from 1 to 25. Most defendants breached conditions on one (n=86, 59%) or two (n=31, 21%) occasions. The mean number of breaches was 3.05. The highest number of breaches was of electronically monitored curfew conditions (n=125).[9] This is likely to result from the accuracy and certainty of detection and the electronic records kept by G4S rather than reflecting reality of the mix of conditions which were breached. For these reasons, it probably provides the most accurate estimate of breach rates.[10]

Outcomes of first breaches were only available for 129 cases. A fifth (n=29, 22%) of defendants were remanded in custody. The highest proportion were re-bailed to the EBS either with the same conditions (n=72, 56%) or with different conditions (n=11, 9%). A tenth (n=14, 11%) of defendants were re-bailed without bail support conditions and in three cases no action was taken. The chances of being remanded in custody on subsequent breaches was higher with over half (n=42, 56%) of these breaches resulting in custodial remands, although a significant minority (n=31, 41%) of defendants were re-bailed with bail support conditions.

Alleged offending while on bail

EBS staff were not routinely alerted to defendants being charged with offences committed while on bail so the extent of alleged offending on bail was likely to be underestimated. Nearly a third (n=194, 30%) of defendants were known to have been charged with offences committed while on the EBS. Most defendants were charged with one set of offences (n=158, 81%).[11] Table 7.1 shows the offences with which defendants were charged, where available. The highest number of alleged offences was theft-related. However a significant number of alleged offences were violence and a relatively high proportion of these appeared to be related to domestic violence incidents. The mean time from the start of bail periods to alleged offending was 42 days.[12]

Table 7.1 Alleged offences committed on bail

	Number
Fraud, theft-related and deception	45
Burglary	15
Violence	15
Battery	12
Breach injunction/restraining order	9
Criminal damage	8
Breach of ASBO	8
Drugs	7
Car crime	7
Common assault	6
Driving offences	5
Serious public order	5
Other	10
Total	**152**

In terms of outcomes, on the first occasion when defendants had allegedly offended on bail, nearly half (n=85, 47%) of defendants were remanded in custody, suggesting that alleged offending on bail was dealt with more harshly by the courts than breaches of bail conditions. However, the same proportion (n=86, 47%) of defendants were re-bailed with bail support with a further four defendants being bailed without bail support conditions. The custodial remand rate might be expected to be higher on subsequent occasions when defendants were accused of offending on bail. However, this was not the case,[13] which suggests that while the EBS may have been used as a last resort and an alternative to custodial remands in some cases, in others (probably around half) it may not have been used in this way.

Failure to appear for court hearings

Failure to appear at court hearings is likely to be under-recorded because EBS staff would not necessarily be aware that defendants had failed to attend. There was no mechanism for the courts to alert EBS staff when defendants failed to appear. For this reason data are presented for the purposes of indicating outcomes when defendants failed to appear at court rather than as an accurate measure of the extent of the problem. A total of 48 defendants were recorded as failing to appear at court on one occasion only. Outcomes were available in 40 cases. They show that over half (n=22, 55%) of defendants who failed to appear while on the EBS were remanded in custody, and under a third (30%) were re-bailed with (n=11) or without (n=1) bail support.

Bail variations

In 165 cases defendants applied for their bail to be varied in some way although this is likely to be an underestimate because the EBS would not necessarily be informed of these applications. Most (n=145) of the applications were granted. In 79 cases, successful applications were made to remove bail support conditions. The mean time for removal of bail support conditions was 79 days.[14] A total of 90 applications were made for changes to residence conditions. The majority of these (n=67) applications related to accommodation provided by the EBS and 59 were known to have been granted.[15]

Case outcomes

Table 7.2 shows the court outcomes for defendants on the EBS. It demonstrates that nearly a quarter (n=82, 23%) of defendants received custodial sentences at the conclusion of their cases.[16] A further 16% (n=60) cases resulted in suspended sentences being imposed.[17] The highest proportion of defendants (n=124, 35%) received a community order.[18] Most suspended sentences (n=26) and community orders (n=60) had one requirement attached, although a significant minority of both orders (n=58) had two or three conditions attached to them. Comparisons with national statistics suggest that offenders sentenced after being on the EBS were more likely to have a community order or suspended sentences imposed than offenders who were bailed and remanded in custody (Home Office, 2008). In terms of custodial sentences, offenders who had been on the EBS were less likely to have custodial sentences imposed than defendants who were remanded in custody while awaiting trial, but more likely to have a custodial sentence imposed than offenders who were bailed (Home Office, 2008).

While it is difficult to be certain because cases change over their lifetime and bail decisions are made very early on in the investigation process, case outcomes provide some indication of whether bail support was diverting defendants from custodial remands. Around 40% of defendants were sentenced to custody (either immediate or suspended), suggesting that bail support was being targeted accurately for this group. By contrast, the number of defendants who eventually received a discharge, a binding-over order, or charged a fine suggests that some net-widening may have occurred.

Additionally, the proportion of cases which were withdrawn is also noteworthy and of some concern and suggests that bail support conditions are sometimes used in cases where evidence is weak.

Table 7.2 Court outcomes for defendants on the EBS[19]

Outcome	N	%
Custody	82	23
Suspended sentence	60	17
Community order	124	35
Deferred sentence	4	1
Fine	9	3
Conditional/absolute discharge/bind over	22	6
Case withdrawn	48	13
Acquitted	9	3
Total	**358**	**100**

Notes

[1]   Forty-seven defendants breached bail support and 27 defendants were known to have breached other bail conditions.

[2]   The mean time to breaches of bail support was 31 days, ranging from 0 to 239 days, whereas the mean time to breach of other conditions was 30 days, ranging from 0 to 373 days.

[3]   Ranging from 0 to 216 days.

[4]   The mean time to breach for EBS was 31 days, ranging from 0 to 373 days. The mean time to breach for other bail conditions was 30 days, ranging from 0 to 239 days.

[5]   41 defendants breached bail support on two occasions, nine defendants breached on three occasions and one defendant breached bail support four times.

[6]   11 breaches were recorded as non-compliant.

[7]   The rest of the group were either sentenced (n=7), remanded in custody on other matters (n=4) or not yet dealt with (n=16).

[8]   The one defendant who breached bail support on four occasions was remanded in custody on his last breach appearance.

[9]   A range of other conditions were breached, most commonly no contact conditions (n=27), exclusion areas (n=18), curfews (n=18) and reporting (n=12).

[10]   G4S only identified around two-thirds of cases, however, where EM was imposed resulting in some cases of breaches not being recorded or notified to the EBS. This is likely to result in breaches of EM being under-recorded.

[11]   Twenty-five defendants were charged with two sets of offences. A further ten defendants were charged with three sets of offences and one defendant was charged with five sets of offences.

[12]   Ranging from 0 to 216 days.

[13] Two-fifths (n=16, 40%) of defendants were remanded in custody at the time they were accused of offending on bail on a second or third occasion, compared with over half (58%) who were re-bailed with bail support (n=21) or without bail support (n=2).

[14] Ranging from 4 to 380 days.

[15] 33 applications related to other conditions including curfews (n=20), no contact conditions (n=6), exclusion conditions (n=3) and reporting (n=4).

[16] The length of custodial sentences ranged from 14 days to five years. Over two-fifths (n=35, 43%) of custodial sentences were 12 months or less.

[17] Over half (n=32, 53%) of these were for a period of 12 months or less.

[18] Two-fifths (n=49, 40%) were for 12 months.

[19] It includes four defendants who were breached or allegedly committed offences on bail. Thirty-one cases were still current at the time data were collected.

Conclusions

8

The chapter summarises the main findings of the evaluation and draws some conclusions about the future of bail support schemes for adults.

Take-up and caseloads

A total of 655 defendants were supervised by the EBS scheme up until the end of June 2008. The take-up rate, in terms of the proportion of EBS proposals made to courts, was quite high. However, the EBS did not meet its target of 600 commencements per year outlined in the original bid to the Treasury Invest to Save Budget (ISB). Some of the defendants on the scheme were likely to have been destined for a custodial remand suggesting that bail support schemes can divert defendants from custody. There are indications that there may be some scope for increasing numbers on the scheme by widening the criteria by which defendants are selected so that the number of proposals made to courts increases. The risk of this approach is that net-widening will occur. There is already some evidence that the EBS was used for defendants who would not otherwise have been remanded in custody. The evidence comes from a number of sources. First, some defendants on the EBS were charged with less serious offences which would not normally result in custodial remands. Second, a proportion of the defendants on the scheme had limited offending and bail histories. Third, a significant number of defendants were re-bailed to the EBS after alleged offending on bail or breaching conditional bail including EBS. Fourth, a significant minority of the sentences imposed were fines or discharges. The high proportion of defendants subject to the EBS charged with domestic violence related offences also raises issues of net-widening. In many of these cases the main, and potentially, the only bail-related issue for the courts is whether an address can be found for the defendants away from where the alleged offence took place. This provides one indication, of several, that defendants may be subject to the EBS simply to provide bail addresses. Consequently, up-tariffing is a risk whereby any subsequent offending or breaches are more likely to result in custodial remands. The original ISB bid recognised that some net-widening was likely to occur, but these findings raise questions about the extent to which it happened and what an acceptable level might be.

One particular mechanism for increasing take-up would be to enable Restriction on Bail (RoB) and bail support conditions to be imposed simultaneously. Working more closely with the Drug Interventions Programme (DIP) would also ensure that the high number of defendants on bail support schemes would receive assistance with their drug use and that defendants on RoB could receive support with other areas of their lives (see Hucklesby et al, 2007). The lack of liaison with the DIP was the most visible but not the only indication that the EBS was bolted on to rather than integrated with existing pre-trial services. This resulted in the fragmentation of bail services leading to duplication and gaps in service provision. There is also evidence of confusion among court decision-makers about the role of the different services and what they offered defendants and the courts as well as duplication in the information they received from different services (see Hucklesby et al, 2007). The situation highlights one of the challenges of having a variety of providers involved in one area of service provision which is the model currently being proposed by the coalition government (Ministry of Justice, 2010d).

The evaluation raises questions about how effectively bail support schemes divert female and BME defendants from custody. It may have been expected that the EBS would have diverted a larger proportion of women from custodial remands given recent concerns about the use of custodial remands for women (see Home Office, 2007) and the fact that women usually have less serious offending and bail histories and are more likely to be charged with less serious offences (Ministry of Justice, 2010e). However, women were still being remanded in custody suggesting that there may have been further scope to divert women from custody. Bringing to an end the separation between bail support and RoB may improve the take-up of bail support for female defendants. The potential drawback of this approach is that defendants become overburdened with appointments. Joint working rather than simply having two schemes running alongside each other should militate against this possibility. A second strategy for increasing the number of women in bail support schemes is to ensure that any barriers, such as a lack of childcare provision and court decision-makers' views about what is appropriate for women, are minimised. While the Partnership Board regularly discussed the number of women in the EBS, it was not apparent that any particular attention had been paid to how bail support could have been tailored to women's circumstances or needs. An equality impact study was undertaken towards the end of the evaluation period but it did not lead to visible changes in practice or procedures. Surprisingly, there was also no evidence of consultation or collaboration with the Together Women Project which was running in the area at the time of the EBS pilot providing specialist advice and assistance to women who had offended or were at risk of offending (Hedderman et al, 2008). Similar issues arise in terms of increasing the representation of BME groups on bail support schemes. Given the high representation of BME defendants in the prison remand population, their numbers on the EBS would have been expected to be higher. Data suggest a number of reasons for the relatively low representation of women and BME defendants on the EBS, but exploring these was hampered by small sample sizes.

The typical defendant on the EBS scheme was male, in his mid-20s and white. The range of offences with which the typical defendant was charged were diverse, but offences of battery, burglary and serious violence together made up just under half of the offences with which defendants were charged. Domestic violence was a feature of many of the offences. Defendants on the EBS had less serious offending and bail histories than defendants who were remanded in custody after proposals for EBS were rejected. Police and CPS views about the defendants' suitability for bail also had an impact on whether defendants were bailed to the scheme. Given previous research findings indicating that the CPS are the crucial agency involved in remand decisions (Hucklesby, 1997a), ensuring that they and the police are aware of the existence of bail support schemes and are the recipients of bail information reports is likely to increase the likelihood that defendants will be diverted from custody. However, the ability of bail information reports to influence the CPS's decisions to object to bail has been diminished by the introduction of Associate Prosecutors in some remand courts. These posts are filled by non-lawyers whose decision-making powers are limited. They do not have the power to change decisions once cases have been discussed with their supervising lawyer without seeking further advice. This has implications for the information/bail support process because the CPS is unlikely to change its decision to object to bail as a result of receiving a bail information report.[1] Consequently, bail information schemes need to engage with the CPS at an earlier stage, when the charging decision is being made, in order to have an impact on their decisions to oppose bail.

Despite lower than expected take-up, the caseload of the EBS was higher than originally envisaged because defendants spent longer on the scheme than anticipated. This may indicate that courts were dealing less expeditiously with cases because defendants were receiving support and assistance. This is potentially a worrying development with costs for defendants, the EBS and the criminal justice process and should be monitored closely. The higher than expected caseloads resulted in capacity problems and raised concerns among EBS managers about any decision to broaden out the criteria to include more defendants in the scheme or to publicise the scheme to attract higher numbers onto it. Caseloads were unevenly distributed between areas, so capacity issues arose in only some areas and were caused by staff resources being in the wrong place rather than a lack of them. Resources need to be deployed flexibly according to actual and expected caseloads rather than staffing levels being the same in each of the six main courts, which was the case for the period covered by this report.

The provision of accommodation is an important element of the EBS with just over two-fifths of defendants being housed by the scheme. This figure is higher than envisaged in the ISB bid. Data indicate that EBS accommodation may have been used unnecessarily for defendants who already had stable accommodation, resulting in net-widening and wasted resources. It was not always clear that accommodated defendants required the support element of the scheme. This might be particularly relevant in cases where defendants had little or no history of previous offending but lacked a suitable bail address. In such circumstances, supplying accommodation only would be less resource intensive and cheaper. Questions were also raised about the suitability of accommodation provided by the EBS, particularly in terms of the high use of bed and breakfast and whether the courts would expect this type of accommodation to be used. Shared accommodation caused logistical and practical difficulties and was costly because it increased the number of unoccupied bed spaces.

Some courts utilised EBS accommodation much more than others suggesting that court cultures may be a factor in the take-up of accommodation (see Hucklesby, 1997b; Paterson and Whittaker, 1994). The number of defendants who continued to be housed in EBS accommodation after bail support periods had ended was relatively high. An important contributory factor in this was the short-hold tenancies provided by the scheme. Move-on accommodation was not always available with the effect that EBS accommodation was unavailable for other defendants.

Working with defendants

Defendants reported that the EBS had helped them to comply with the requirements of their bail and had helped them deal with their problems. Most defendants on the scheme had their needs assessed. Their needs mirrored closely the typical needs identified in offender populations (SEU, 2002). Most defendants received the minimum number of contacts with the EBS, but there it was not always evident that defendants were provided with targeted, structured support which dealt with their specific needs. Some defendants did not have three contacts a week with the EBS and a significant minority of contacts were by telephone, raising concerns about the concordance between the expectations of the courts and the reality of what EBS provided. This has the capacity to affect the credibility of bail support schemes in the eyes of the courts, the public and defendants. It is suggested that bail support schemes should be more transparent about the services they provide and the nature of the contacts with defendants. Procedures to assess the risks posed by defendants were applied inconsistently, potentially leaving EBS staff and mentors in vulnerable situations.

There was evidence that EBS staff were actively liaising and referring defendants to other agencies. This suggests that defendants' problems were starting to be addressed and that staff were mindful that other agencies were involved with defendants and that they were unable to deal with all the issues with which defendants presented. However, one area where contact was limited was providing feedback to the court while defendants were on the EBS and during the sentencing process. The lack of information available to the court from the EBS in terms of defendants' compliance reduces the potential for their behaviour while on the EBS to be considered by those passing sentences. Positive information from the EBS may reduce the likelihood of a custodial sentence being imposed.

Mentoring by volunteers was an integral part of the original proposal for the scheme. It contributed to the EBS by providing support for defendants over and above that offered by paid staff. However, the mentoring component of the EBS was slow to take off and take-up was lower than planned, resulting in many defendants having little or no contact with mentors. By contrast, a relatively small proportion of defendants had sustained contact with mentors, which suggests that mentoring may be a valuable, but potentially costly, asset to bail support schemes. It also raises questions about whether this is appropriate, the opportunity cost of this support and whether it is an effective use of a scarce resource. With government intentions to increase the role of volunteers in the criminal justice process (Cabinet Office, 2010; Number10. gov.uk, 2010), the EBS provides evidence of some of the issues which may arise. For example, whether volunteers should be used to supplement or as a substitute for the input of paid staff, whether volunteers should be expected to report non-compliance and how this might work in practice, how to manage heightened concerns about risk for both defendants and volunteers and holding mentors to account particularly when they fail to turn up for appointments with defendants. The experience of the EBS also demonstrates that setting up and running a volunteer mentoring service has considerable costs in terms of staff time and resources.

Differences between areas

There were differences in take-up of the EBS, variations in the use of additional bail conditions such as electronic monitoring and EBS accommodation between areas and differences in the extent to which defendants were likely to have been diverted from custody. Some of the variations in take-up are explainable in terms of the courts in urban areas having a larger pool of potential candidates because they operated in busier courts. Remand courts in these areas were also presided over by District Judges who had greater knowledge of, and confidence in, the scheme (Hucklesby et al, 2008). However, it is unlikely that either of these factors fully explain the differences found and that court cultures were an important determinant of take-up of the scheme (see Hucklesby, 1997b; Paterson and Whittaker, 1994).

Despite the EBS being a regional scheme with shared policies and procedures, divergent working practices were apparent between areas. Of particular concern was the different practices in terms of the number of contacts per week, but some areas did not appear to be following EBS procedures more generally. Local working cultures appeared to have formed resulting in defendants having different experiences of the EBS and the obligations it placed on them both of which threatened the credibility of, and confidence in, the EBS and raised issues of fairness and justice. The regional nature of the scheme also caused considerable logistical difficulties and made managing the project challenging. The main advantage of a regional scheme was that defendants could be required by the courts to reside in an area away from where their offending took place.

Outcomes

Findings relating to outcomes are tentative because they rely on data collected by the EBS rather than official sources. Three-fifths of defendants were known by the scheme to have either breached bail or be charged with offending on bail. Half of the defendants were known to have breached bail conditions with a quarter of this group breaching bail support, half breaching bail support only and a third breaching other bail conditions. Overall, a third (n=208) of defendants breached bail support. Nearly a third of defendants were known to have been charged with an offence committed while bailed to the EBS. Some defendants were remanded in custody as a result of breaches of EBS, other bail conditions or alleged offending on bail, but a significant proportion were re-bailed.

One of the implicit aims of the EBS was to reduce the use of custodial sentences through enabling defendants to demonstrate that they could comply with the restrictions of the scheme. There was some evidence that it had been successful in this regard although the probable existence of a net-widening effect of the EBS muddies the picture. Defendants sentenced after being on the EBS were more likely to receive a community order or a suspended sentence than offenders who were bailed or remanded in custody and less likely to have a custodial sentence imposed than defendants remanded in custody (Home Office, 2008). In terms of case outcomes, nearly a quarter of defendants received custodial sentences at the conclusion of their cases with a further 16% of cases resulting in suspended sentences. Over a third of defendants received community orders. A significant minority of defendants received discharges, binding-over orders and fines or cases were withdrawn raising concerns over mis-targeting of the EBS.

The EBS had no consistent exit strategy. It could be assumed that defendants who received a custodial or community sentence were likely to receive continued assistance from the prison and/or probation services. However, a large number of defendants received other non-custodial sentences, were acquitted or had their cases withdrawn. In these circumstances, support was usually removed immediately whatever the wishes of defendants although some defendants who were accommodated were supported for a short period by EBS accommodation officers. The sudden removal of contact has the potential to destabilise individuals and to undo any positive work which had been done while subject to bail support. For these reasons, bail support schemes should ensure that they have an exit strategy and that the necessary support is in place for defendants who leave the scheme at the end of their bail period.

The EBS theoretically involved the same level of contacts for all defendants whatever the circumstances or the length of time they were on the scheme. There was no mechanism to increase or decrease the number of contacts as a way of rewarding compliance or dealing with non-compliance or variations in bail risks over time. Introducing flexibility to the provision of bail support may increase its attractiveness to the courts, enable it to cater for a wider range of defendants, act as an exit strategy and increase compliance (Bottoms, 2001). On the other hand, flexibility may result in inconsistencies and increase the mismatch between the reality of being on a bail support scheme and the expectations of the courts, reducing the credibility of schemes.

The future of bail support schemes

Recently, the coalition government has indicated that it plans to reduce the prison population by 3,000 and that part of the decrease will be in the remand population (Ministry of Justice, 2010d). One of the chosen mechanisms for achieving the reduction is to restrict the use of custodial remands for offences which are unlikely to result in defendants being imprisoned if they are convicted. According to official figures, progress has already been made in this regard with a higher proportion of defendants who were remanded in custody being imprisoned than previously (see Chapter One and Ministry of Justice, 2010d). However, such figures need to be treated with caution because they are just as likely to be explained by sentencers increasing the use of custodial sentences for offenders who were remanded in custody than by a decrease in the use of remand in custody for defendants who are unlikely to be sentenced to imprisonment. It is also difficult to predict which defendants might receive a custodial sentence when cases are dynamic and change over time. Bail support schemes generally and the Bail Accommodation and Support Scheme particularly are not explicitly referred to in the Green Paper (Ministry of Justice, 2010d). However, the EBS demonstrates that they have the potential to assist the government to meet its target. Using bail support schemes as a mechanism to reduce the prison remand population is not without costs. Bail support schemes have to be properly resourced. They may be cheaper than custodial remands but only if take-up and compliance is high and they are targeted accurately. Bail support schemes need to demonstrate that they are a viable and cost effective measure especially at a time when all publically funded services are required to provide 'more for less'. Unfortunately, the evidence base is weak particularly because the Ministry of Justice decided not to fund the second phase of the EBS evaluation which would have begun to address such issues.

Economic factors are not the only relevant consideration when deciding on the future of bail support schemes. Normative judgements need to be made about whether, and to what extent, net-widening is acceptable in order to divert some defendants from custodial remands. Questions such as whether it is acceptable that some defendants are required to comply with a strict regime of appointments and be subject to more monitoring than necessary in order for other defendants to avoid spending time in custody while awaiting trial. Such judgements have to be made bearing in mind that the people in question are legally innocent. Also relevant to such considerations is whether defendants on the bail support schemes should have the opportunity to receive support and assistance with issues and problems they are facing. Whether this militates against the fact that they are legally innocent is open to question. Theoretically, schemes which work with defendants should not work on issues linked to offending because it is not proven that defendants have committed an offence. In reality, however, there is often little or no distinction between defendants' needs and criminogenic needs. As one interviewee said in this study, it is often the case that the work which bail support schemes do prepares defendants for post-sentence interventions. Yet, this perspective presumes that defendants will be convicted, going against the letter and principle of the law. An alternative purpose for bail support schemes, which fits with the legal status of defendants, is for them to have a solely monitoring and controlling function. This chimes with the views of many of the interviewees who saw monitoring and control as the primary function of the EBS. It was largely the employees of the EBS who believed that they should be working to ameliorate defendants' needs and who were frustrated by the lack of opportunities to do this type of work. Further divergences of opinion were apparent in relation to whether the EBS was aiming to reduce offending in the long term or to focus on enhancing short-term compliance with bail conditions. Such discrepancies in views about the purpose of bail support schemes highlight the nebulous nature of bail support (Drakeford et al, 2001; Cavadino and Gibson, 1993) and the need for a debate about what they should be aiming to do. This conversation might also encompass an examination of whether bail support is the most appropriate term for the service provided or whether bail supervision – which has been used in the past by the Youth Justice Board (Allen and Maynard, 2008), in Scotland (Paterson, 1996) and in Northern Ireland (NIO, 1996) – may be a more accurate description of their purpose and the work they undertake.

Single initiatives such as the EBS or the BASS are to be welcomed because they should divert some defendants from custody and may reduce the prison remand population. But their impact is likely to be small and/or temporary partly because funding is often short-term and limited. They also struggle for public credibility in the climate of popular punitiveness, the drift towards greater punitiveness and concerns about public safety which have resulted in perennial calls to remand more defendants in custody (Garland, 2001; Pratt et al, 2005). Despite the apparent usefulness of bail support schemes to divert defendants from custody, their introduction needs to be considered systematically and not as a knee-jerk reaction to increasing prison populations. A policy of diversion should not be at any cost because of the implications for defendants including restrictions on their liberty and a heightened likelihood of non-compliance. It is important not to lose sight of the fact that defendants are legally innocent and should be required to abide by the minimum restrictions to meet the bail risk posed. The ad hoc, often rushed and uncoordinated introduction of new schemes should be avoided. A more considered approach is likely to be more effective (Mair and Lloyd, 1996). This could encompass a remand management strategy which would provide a considered, strategic and coordinated approach to dealing with the risks posed by defendants awaiting trial while also aiming to keep the use of custodial remands to a minimum and include law, policy and practice. A potentially interesting development within this overall strategy would be to implement a case management approach to bail, mirroring what is available post-sentence, whereby courts would have a range of options including bail support, drug and alcohol services and mental health provision from which to select conditions which would then be managed by a bail worker. This would avoid the pitfalls of bolt-on schemes. A danger is that defendants would be overloaded with requirements but the experience of the generic community sentence suggests that this might not be the case (Mair et al, 2007; Ministry of Justice, 2010b). The first step towards a strategic approach must be to increase the woefully inadequate information about the operation of the remand process which is currently collated and published (Hucklesby, 2009).

The government has signalled its intention to increase the role of the voluntary sector in the provision of criminal justice services as part of its 'Big Society' agenda (Ministry of Justice, 2010d). The experience of the EBS adds to the weight of the already significant amount of evidence that the voluntary sector is able to provide services in the criminal justice system and to work alongside criminal justice professionals (see, for example, Carey and Walker, 2002). Nonetheless, a number of issues arose with the EBS pilot which have implications for the voluntary sector being involved in criminal justice services beyond the provision of bail support schemes. First, providing the EBS as a standalone service was relatively expensive and could not produce economies of scale available to an organisation such as probation areas/trusts. For example, a whole management structure was required to deliver one service rather than a range of services. Second, the service lacked flexibility. Peaks and troughs in demand for the service were not easily dealt with because there were no additional staff available when the scheme was busy or tasks for EBS staff to perform when it was not. Three, the EBS used the premises of statutory agencies (the courts and Probation Service) without reimbursement. While such arrangements were necessary for the smooth operation of the scheme, it meant that statutory services subsidised the EBS and the costs were not accounted for. Four, credibility was also 'borrowed' from the Probation Service because many interviewees believed that the EBS was part of the Probation Service. How much this had an impact on the success of the scheme is not clear, but voluntary sector organisations may have to work harder to earn the respect of the courts and criminal justice agencies without the clout of an established criminal justice agency behind them.

Payment by results is an integral part of the coalition government's policy of increasing voluntary sector involvement in service provision (Ministry of Justice, 2010d). In order for this policy to succeed, organisations will be required to keep robust records of their activities. They will be required to ensure that they have effective IT programmes for recording their work and outcomes. The experience of the EBS suggests that this is not always a priority for voluntary sector organisations and their workers who often prefer to concentrate on the 'real' work with defendants or offenders (Hucklesby and Worrall, 2007).

Notes

[1] Associate Prosecutors are required to follow the advice given to them by CPS lawyers who review cases prior to court, usually at the police station. Associate Prosecutors have no power to change the decisions subsequently without consulting a CPS lawyer, which involves asking the court to stand down cases. Most Associate Prosecutors reported that they would be reluctant to ask for this to happen because their request was unlikely to be granted.

References

Airs, J., Elliott, R. and Conrad, E. (2000) *Electronically monitored curfew as a condition of bail – report of a pilot*, RDS Occasional Paper, London: Home Office.

Allen, R. and Maynard, W. (2008) 'Bail supervision and support', *On track*, London: Youth Justice Board.

Ares, C.E., Rankin, A. and Sturz, H.J. (1963) 'The Manhattan Bail Project: an interim report on the use of pre-trial release', *New York University Law Review*, vol 38, pp 38–67.

Ashworth, A. (1992) *Sentencing and criminal justice*, London: Weidenfeld and Nicolson.

Avon and Somerset Constabulary (1991) *The effect of 'reoffending' on bail on crime in Avon and Somerset*, Bristol: Avon and Somerset Constabulary.

Barry, M., Malloch, M., Moodie, K., Nellis, M., Knapp, M., Romeo, R. and Dhanasiri, S. (2007) *An evaluation of the use of electronic monitoring as a condition of bail in Scotland*, Edinburgh: Scottish Executive.

Bottomley, A.K. (1968) 'The granting of bail: principles and practice', *Modern Law Review*, vol 31, pp 40–54.

Bottomley, A.K. (1970) *Prison before trial*, Occasional Paper in Social Administration, No. 39, London: Bell and Son.

Bottoms, A. (2001) 'Compliance and community penalties', in A. Bottoms, L. Gelsthorpe and S. Rex (eds) *Community penalties: Change and challenges*, Cullompton: Willan Publishing.

Brown, I. and Hullin, R. (1993) 'Contested bail applications: The treatment of ethnic minority and white offenders', *Criminal Law Review*, February, pp 107–13.

Brown, I., Harris, R., Cocker, S., Ramsden, J., Robinson, E. and Chana, R. (2008) 'Evaluation of the Bail Information Pathfinder: Yorkshire and Humberside', *Research Review*, 37, Wakefield: West Yorkshire Probation Area.

Burnett, R. and Eaton, G. (2004) *Factors associated with effective practice in approved premises*, Home Office Online Report 65/04, London: Home Office.

Burrows, J., Henderson, P. and Morgan, P. (1994) *Improving bail decisions: The Bail Process Project, Phase 1*, Research and Planning Unit Paper 90, London: Home Office.

Cabinet Office (2010) *Big Society – Overview* at www.cabinetoffice.gov.uk/content/big-society-overview

Carey, M. and Walker, R. (2002) 'The penal voluntary sector', in S. Bryans, C. Martin and R. Walker (eds) *Prisons and the voluntary sector*, Winchester: Waterside Press.

Carter, P. (2003) *Managing offenders, reducing crime: A new approach*, London: Home Office and PM Strategy Unit.

Cavadino, P. and Gibson, B. (1993) *Bail: The law, best practice and the debate*, Winchester: Waterside Press.

De Haas, E. (1940) *Antiquities of bail*, New York: Morningside Heights.

Doherty, M. and East, R. (1985) 'Bail decisions in magistrates' courts', *British Journal of Criminology*, vol 25, pp 251–66.

Doward, J. (2008) 'Warning over backlash in bail hostel row', *Observer*, 10 August.

Drakeford, M., Haines, K., Cotton, B. and Octigan, M. (2001) *Pre-trial services and the future of probation*, Cardiff: University of Wales Press.

Fiddes, C. (1989) 'Bail information schemes', *Probation Journal*, vol 36, no 2, pp 74–7.

Garland, D. (2001) *The culture of control: Crime and social order in contemporary society*, Chicago: University of Chicago Press.

Godson, D. and Mitchell, C. (1991) *Bail information schemes in English Magistrates' Courts*, London: Inner London Probation Service

Greater Manchester Police (1988) *Offences committed on bail*, Research Paper, Manchester: Greater Manchester Police.

Haines, K. and Octigan, M. (1999) *Reducing remand in custody: The probation and remand services*, London: Association of Chief Officers of Probation.

Hansard (2009a) *Bail Accommodation and Support Service: Written answer*, Hansard 3 February 2009, Column 1162W.

Hansard (2009b) Written answer to Mr Grieve 2 February 2009 at www.publications. parliament.uk/pa/cm200809/cmhansrd/cm090202/text/90202w0013.htm

Hansard (2010) *Bail Accommodation and Support Service: Written answer*, Hansard 11 January 2010, Column 785W.

Harris, R. and Robinson, E. (2008) *Evaluation of the Bail Information Pathfinder in Yorkshire and Humberside*, Wakefield, National Probation Service (West Yorkshire) at www.westyorksprobation.org.uk/deliverfile.php?id=155

Hedderman, C., Palmer, E. and Hollin, C. (2008) *Implementing services for women offenders and those 'at risk' of offending: Action research with Together Women*, Ministry of Justice Research Series 12/08.

HMIP (Her Majesty's Inspector of Prisons) (2000) *Unjust deserts: A thematic review by the HM Chief Inspector of Prisons of the treatment and conditions for unsentenced prisoners in England and Wales*, London: Home Office.

HMIPro (Her Majesty's Inspector of Probation) (2000) *Towards race equality: A thematic inspection*, London: Home Office.

HMIPro (1993) *Bail information: Report of the thematic inspection*, London: Home Office.

Home Office (1974) *Bail procedures in magistrates' courts: Report of a working party*, London: HMSO.

Home Office (1989) *Prison statistics England and Wales 1988*, Cmnd 847, HMSO: London.

Home Office (1993) *Prison statistics England and Wales 1991*, Cmnd 2157, HMSO, London.

Home Office (2000) *Bail information*, Probation Circular 29/2000, London: Home Office.

Home Office (2005) *Bail information schemes*, Probation Circular 19/2005, London: Home Office.

Home Office (2007) *The Corston report: A review of women with particular vulnerabilities in the criminal justice system*, London: Home Office.

Home Office (2008) *Criminal statistics England and Wales 2007*, London: Home Office.

Hucklesby, A. (1994a) 'The use and abuse of conditional bail', *Howard Journal*, vol 33, no 3, pp 258–70.

Hucklesby, A. (1994b) *Bail or jail: The magistrates' decision*, unpublished PhD thesis, University of Glamorgan.

Hucklesby, A. (1996) 'Bail or jail? The practical operation of the Bail Act 1976', *Journal of Law and Society*, vol 23, no 2, pp 213–33.

Hucklesby, A. (1997a) 'Remand decision makers', *Criminal Law Review*, April: 269–81.

Hucklesby, A. (1997b) 'Court culture: An explanation of variations in the use of bail in magistrates' courts', *Howard Journal*, vol 36, no 2 (May), pp 129–45.

Hucklesby, A. (2001) 'Police bail and the use of conditions', *Criminal Justice*, vol 1, no 4, pp 441–64.

Hucklesby, A. (2002) 'Bail in criminal cases', in M. McConville and G. Wilson (eds) *Handbook of the criminal justice process*, Oxford: Oxford University Press, pp 115–36.

Hucklesby, A. (2009) 'Keeping the lid on the prison remand population', *Current Issues in Criminal Justice*, vol 21, no 1, pp 3–23.

Hucklesby, A. (2010) 'Pre-trial initiatives', in A. Hucklesby and E. Wincup (eds) *Drug interventions in criminal justice*, Buckingham: Open University Press.

Hucklesby, A. and Marshall, E. (2000) 'Tackling offending on bail', *Howard Journal*, vol 39, no 2 (May), pp 150–70.

Hucklesby, A. and Wincup, E. (eds) (2010) *Drug interventions in criminal justice*, Maidenhead: Open University Press.

Hucklesby, A. and Worrall, J. (2007) 'The voluntary sector and prisoners' resettlement', in A. Hucklesby and L. Hagley-Dickinson (eds) *Prisoner resettlement: Policy and practice*, Cullompton: Willan Publishing, pp 174–98.

Hucklesby, A., Eastwood, C., Seddon, T. and Spriggs, A. (2007) *The evaluation of restriction on bail pilots: Final report*, RDS On-line report 06/07, London: Home Office.

Hucklesby, A. Jarrold, K. and Kazantzoglou, E. (2008) *Effective bail scheme evaluation: Action research report*, Unpublished: Ministry of Justice.

Hudson, B. and Bramhall, G. (2005) 'Assessing the "Other": Constructions of "Asianness" in risk assessments by probation officers', *British Journal of Criminology*, vol 45, pp 721–40.

ILPAS (Inner London Probation and Aftercare Service) (1976) *ILPAS/Vera bail project: Report of the first year and proposal for the second year*, London: ILPAS.

James, A., Bottomley, A.K., Liebling, A. and Clare, E. (1997) *Privatizing prisons: Rhetoric and reality*, London: Sage.

King, M. (1971) *Bail or custody?*, London: Cobden Trust.

Kirkup, J. (2008) '150 bail hostels built in secret', *Daily Telegraph*, 30 April.

LGA (Local Government Association) (2009) 'Public given say over bail accommodation locations', Press Release 6 August, www.lga.gov.uk/lga/core/page.do?pageId=2808352

Lloyd, C. (1992) *Bail information schemes: Practice and effect*, Home Office Research and Planning Unit Paper no.69, London: Home Office.

Lobley, D. and Smith, D. (2000) *Evaluation of electronically monitored restriction of liberty order*, Edinburgh: Scottish Executive Central Research Unit.

Mair, G. (1988) *Probation day centres*, Home Office Research Study no100, London: HMSO.

Mair, G. (2009) 'Community sentences', in A. Hucklesby and A. Wahidin (eds) *Criminal justice*, Oxford: Oxford University Press.

Mair, G. and Lloyd, C. (1996) 'Development of bail schemes in England and Wales', in F. Paterson (ed) *Understanding bail in Britain*, Edinburgh: Scottish Office.

Mair, G. and Mortimer, E. (1996) *Curfew orders with electronic monitoring*, Home Office Research Study no 163, London: Home Office.

Mair, G. and Nee, C. (1990) *Electronic monitoring: the trials and their results*, Home Office Research Study no 120, Home Office.

Mair, G., Cross, N. and Taylor, S. (2007) *The use of the community order and the suspended sentence order*, London: Centre for Crime and Justice Studies.

McIvor, G. (1992) *Sentenced to serve: The operation and impact of community service by offenders*. Aldershot: Avebury.

Ministry of Justice (2007) 'New bail accommodation and support scheme', at www.justice.gov.uk/news/newsrelease180607a.htm

Ministry of Justice (2008a) *Offender management caseload statistics 2007*, London: Ministry of Justice.

Ministry of Justice (2008b) *Criminal Justice and Immigration Act 2008* (provisions commencing on 3 November 2008), Circular 2008/05, London: Ministry of Justice at www.justice.gov.uk/publications/docs/circular-criminal-justice–031108.pdf

Ministry of Justice (2009a) *Offender management caseload statistics 2008*, London: Ministry of Justice.

Ministry of Justice (2009b) *Statistics on race and the criminal justice system 2007/8*, London: Ministry of Justice.

Ministry of Justice (2009c) *Total adult caseload pre-trial*, unpublished statistics, Electronic Monitoring Unit, London: Ministry of Justice.

Ministry of Justice (2010a) 'Criminal statistics England and Wales 2009', *Statistics Bulletin*, London: Ministry of Justice at www.justice.gov.uk/criminal-statistics-annual-2009.pdf.

Ministry of Justice (2010b) 'Offender management caseload statistics 2009', *Statistics Bulletin*, London, Ministry of Justice at www.justice.gov.uk/publications/prisonandprobation.htm

Ministry of Justice (2010c) *Population in custody August 2010*, London: Ministry of Justice.

Ministry of Justice (2010d) *Breaking the cycle: Effective punishment, rehabilitation and sentencing of offenders*, Cmnd 7972, London: The Stationary Office.

Ministry of Justice (2010e) *Statistics on women and the criminal justice system 2009/10*, London: Ministry of Justice.

Ministry of Justice (2010f) *Total adult caseload pre-trial*, unpublished statistics, Electronic Monitoring Unit, London: Ministry of Justice.

Morgan, P. (1992) 'Offending on bail: A survey of recent research', Research and Planning Unit Paper 65, London: Home Office.

Morgan, P. and Henderson, P. (1998) *Remand decisions and offending on bail: an evaluation of the Bail Process Project*, Home Office Research Study no 184, London: Home Office.

Morgan, R. and Jones, S. (1992) 'Bail or jail?', E. Stockdale and S. Casale (eds) *Criminal justice under stress*, London: Blackstones, pp 34–63.

NAO (National Audit Office) (2004) *Facing justice: Tackling defendants' non-attendance at court*, London: The Stationary Office.

NIO (Northern Ireland Office) (2006) *Evaluation of bail supervision and support scheme*, Research and Statistical Series Report no 13, Belfast: Northern Ireland Office.

NOMS (National Offender Management Service) (2007) *Effective bail scheme pilot in Yorkshire and Humberside*.

NOMS (2010) 'Bail accommodation and support scheme for bail and HDC: Change of contract', Prison Service Instruction 34/2010.

Northumbria Police (1991) *Bail and multiple offending*, Newcastle: Northumbria Police.

NPS (National Probation Service) (2005a) *Criminal Justice Act 2003: new sentences and the new report framework*, Probation Circular 18/2005, London: Home Office.

NPS (2005b) *Bail information schemes*, Probation Circular 19/2005, London: Home Office.

NPS (2008) *Accommodation and support scheme for bail and HDC*, Briefing no 42, London: Home Office.

NPS (2009a) *Determining pre-sentence report type*, Probation Circular 06/09, London: Home Office.

NPS (2009b) *Pre-sentence report decision tool*, Probation Circular 12/07, London: Home Office.

Number10.gov.uk (2010) Big Society speech, 19 July 2010 at www.number10.gov.uk/news/speeches-and-transcripts/2010/07/big-society-speech-53572

Paterson, F. (ed) (1996) *Understanding bail in Britain*, Edinburgh: The Scottish Office.

Paterson, F. and Whittaker, C. (1994) *Operating bail: Decision-making under the bail etc (Scotland) Act 1980*, Edinburgh: The Scottish Office Central Research Unit.

Phillips, C. and Brown, D. (1998) *Entry into the criminal justice system: A survey of police arrests and their outcomes*, Home Office Research Study no 185, London: Home Office.

Pratt, J., Brown, D., Hallsworth, S. and Morrison, W. (eds) (2005) *The new punitiveness: Trends, theories and perspectives*, Cullompton: Willan Publishing.

Raine, J. and Willson, M. (1994) *Conditional bail or bail with conditions? The use and effectiveness of bail conditions*, Report to the Home Office, unpublished.

Raine, J. and Willson, M. (1996) 'The imposition of conditions in bail decisions', *Howard Journal*, vol 35, no 3, pp 256–70.

SEU (Social Exclusion Unit) (2002) *Reducing reoffending by ex-prisoners*, London: Office of the Deputy Prime Minister.

Stone, C. (1988) *Bail information for the Crown Prosecution Service*, London: Vera Institute of Justice.

Thomas, S. and Hucklesby, A. (2002) *Remand management: Effective practice guide and source document*, London: Youth Justice Board.

Warner, S. and McIvor, G. (1994) *Pre-trial services in Scotland: An evaluation of two experimental Bail Information and Accommodation Schemes*, Edinburgh: Scottish Office Central Research Unit.

Appendix One

Figure AI Process maps of the Effective Bail Scheme

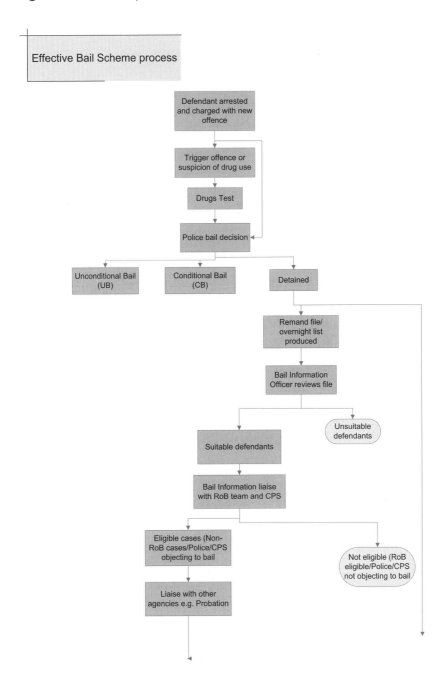

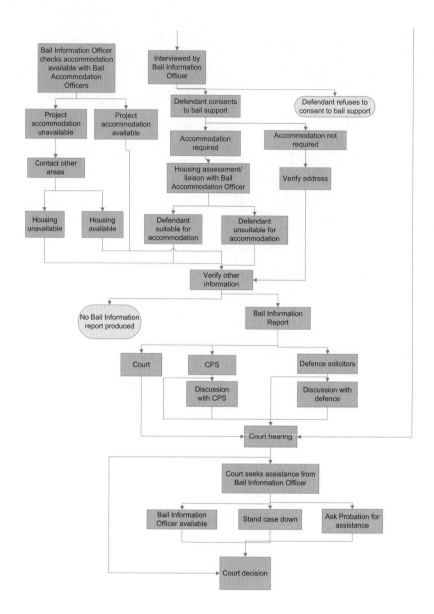

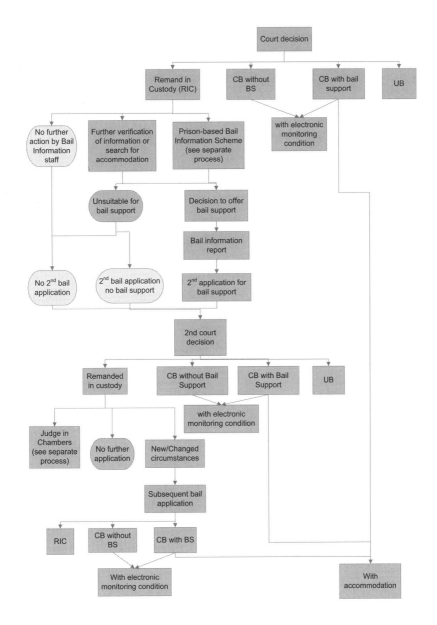

Bail support schemes for adults

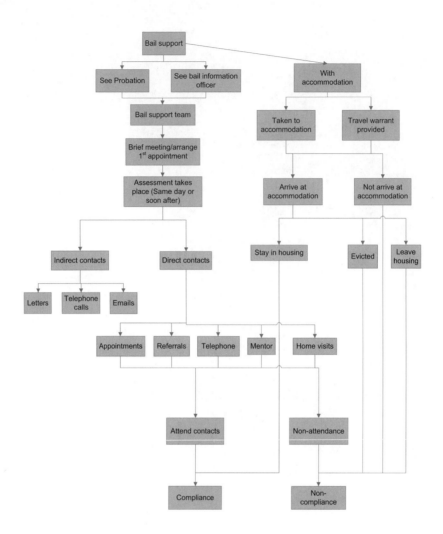

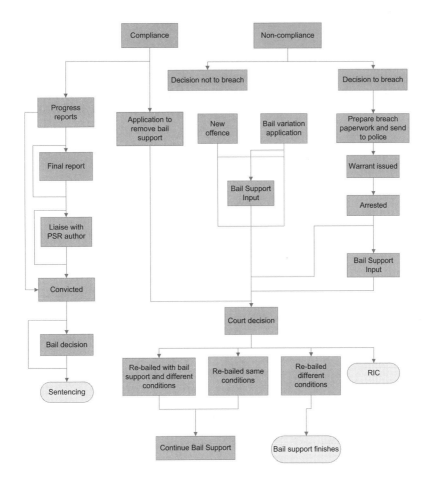

Bail support schemes for adults

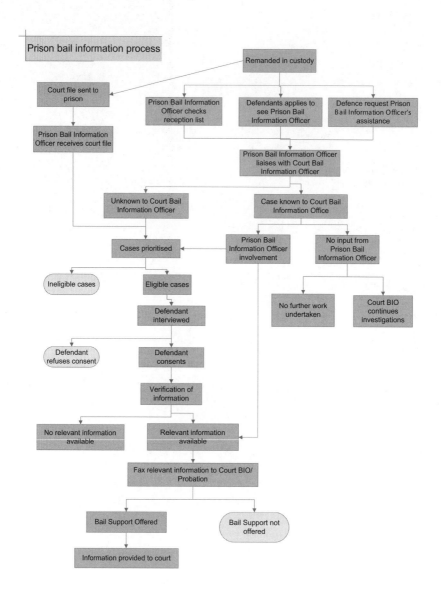

Prison bail information process

Remanded in custody

Court file sent to prison

Prison Bail Information Officer checks reception list

Defendants applies to see Prison Bail Information Officer

Defence request Prison Bail Information Officer's assistance

Prison Bail Information Officer receives court file

Prison Bail Information Officer liaises with Court Bail Information Officer

Unknown to Court Bail Information Officer

Case known to Court Bail Information Office

Cases prioritised

Prison Bail Information Officer involvement

No input from Prison Bail Information Officer

Ineligible cases

Eligible cases

No further work undertaken

Court BIO continues investigations

Defendant interviewed

Defendant refuses consent

Defendant consents

Verification of information

No relevant information available

Relevant information available

Fax relevant information to Court BIO/ Probation

Bail Support Offered

Bail Support not offered

Information provided to court

Judge in Chambers applications

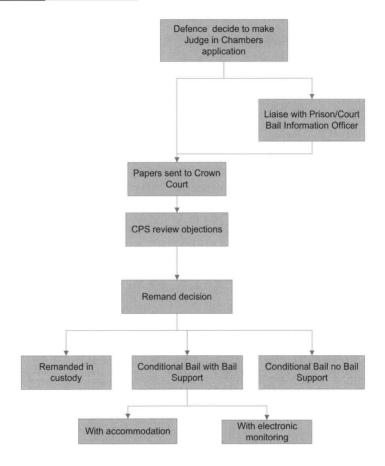

Effective bail scheme process
Prison bail information process
Judge in Chambers applications

Appendix Two

Commencements on the EBS by area

Table A2 Number of commencements on EBS by area

Month	Bradford	Hull	Leeds	Scar.	Sheffield	York	HSN	Total
2006								
Nov	1		6		10			17
Dec	3		4		4			11
2007								
Jan	3		8		5			16
Feb	4	7	8	2	3	2		26
March	6	8	3	3	5	0		25
April	2	2	6	3	4	0		17
May	5	5	3	2	6	1		22
June	7	9	6	7	8	4		41
July	11	5	10	5	14	6		51
Aug	5	7	7	6	8	7		40
Sept	5	9	11	2	11	7		45
Oct	8	11	9	9	9	1		47
Nov	6	8	10	7	3	2		36
Dec	9	5	6	1	9	2	1	33
2008								
Jan	7	10	11	4	8	4	0	44
Feb	5	3	6	3	12	2	1	32
March	2	3	11	5	5	0	0	26
April	7	8	10	2	12	4	7	50
May	3	6	11	5	5	2	0	32
June	4	12	11	4	8	3	2	44
Total	103	118	157	70	149	47	11	655

Appendix Three

EBS caseloads

Table A3 Number of defendants on EBS by area

Month	Bradford	Hull	Leeds	Scar.	Sheffield	York	HSN	Total
2006								
Nov	1	n/a	6	n/a	10	n/a	n/a	17
Dec	4	n/a	10	n/a	14	n/a	n/a	28
2007								
Jan	7	n/a	17	n/a	12	n/a	n/a	36
Feb	10	7	19	2	13	2	n/a	53
March	14	14	16	5	17	2	n/a	68
April	11	14	17	6	15	0	n/a	63
May	12	15	15	4	17	1	n/a	64
June	19	20	18	9	20	5	n/a	91
July	28	18	21	12	25	9	n/a	113
Aug	24	20	24	10	24	16	n/a	118
Sept	18	22	29	8	29	18	n/a	124
Oct	21	24	33	14	30	13	n/a	135
Nov	24	23	30	17	21	9	n/a	124
Dec	25	21	30	12	25	9	1	123
2008								
Jan	27	24	34	11	27	7	1	131
Feb	17	17	30	10	36	6	2	118
March	16	17	36	13	30	4	2	118
April	21	18	39	9	36	7	7	137
May	20	21	35	10	25	8	6	125
June	15	27	40	10	23	8	7	130

Appendix Four

EBS accommodation

Table A4 Number of cases in which defendants were accommodated

	Number	Percentage of cases N=275
Bradford	47	46
Hull	38	32
Leeds	61	39
Scarborough	53	76
Sheffield	41	28
York	27	57
Harrogate, Skipton and Northallerton (HSN)	8	73
All sites	275	42

Appendix Five

Accommodation caseloads

Table A5 Number of defendants in EBS accommodation by area

Month	Bradford	Hull	Leeds	Scar.	Sheffield	York	HSN	Total
2006								
Nov					1			1
Dec	1		2		3			6
2007								
Jan	2		6		5			13
Feb	2	2	7	1	4			16
March	2	5	7	4	7			25
April	3	5	6	3	6			23
May	2	5	5	3	6			21
June	3	5	5	5	5	1		24
July	9	7	7	7	8	3		41
Aug	9	7	11	7	7	6		47
Sept	4	10	13	3	8	6		44
Oct	7	11	12	10	8	8		56
Nov	7	11	12	13	5	5		53
Dec	8	10	11	8	6	6		49
2008								
Jan	8	12	12	7	7	6		52
Feb	7	12	10	5	7	5	1	47
March	7	12	9	9	6	5		48
April	4	13	15	9	9	4	3	57
May	6	10	15	4	6	5	2	48
June	6	12	15	2	7	4	2	48